An Introduction to International Varieties of English

Laurie Bauer

Edinburgh University Press

© Laurie Bauer, 2002

Edinburgh University Press Ltd
22 George Square, Edinburgh

Reprinted 2005, 2007

Typeset in Janson
by Norman Tilley Graphics and
printed and bound in Great Britain
by MPG Books Ltd, Bodmin, Cornwall

A CIP record for this book is available from the British Library

ISBN 0 7486 1337 4 (hardback)
ISBN 0 7486 1338 2 (paperback)

Contents

Acknowledgements

Grateful acknowledgement is made to the following sources for permission to reproduce material in this book previously published elsewhere. Every effort has been made to trace copyright holders, but if any have been inadvertently overlooked the publisher will be pleased to make the necessary arrangement at the first opportunity.

Cambridge University Press and Tom McArthur for Figure 2.4 on p. 22, from McArthur (1987).

Contact, for the text published on 27 February 1992 reproduced on p. 103.

Max Niemeyer Verlag GmbH for Figure 2.3 on p. 21, from Görlach (1990a).

The New Zealand Listener, for the letter to the editor of 12 March 1983 reproduced on p. 102.

Professor D. Throsby for the text from *The Sydney Morning Herald* of 9 August 1999 reproduced on p. 67.

Times Newspapers Limited for Eleanor Mills's Column, *The Sunday Times*, 7 January 2001. © Times Newspapers Limited 2001, reproduced on p. 90.

The author would like to thank Carolin Biewer for searching corpora for data for Chapter 5, and the following people who have commented on earlier drafts: Winifred Bauer, Derek Britton, Jack Chambers, Vivian de Klerk, Manfred Görlach, Edgar Schneider. None of them is responsible for any errors of fact or interpretation.

Abbreviations and conventions used in the text

/…/	enclose a phonemic transcription
[…]	enclose a phonetic transcription, where the actual sounds made are the focus of attention
<…>	enclose an orthographic representation; enclose URLs
FORCE	small capitals indicate lexical sets, see section 6.1
*	not a grammatical sentence/construction
Aus	Australia(n)
CDN	Canada/Canadian
GA	General American, see section 6.1
NAm	North American
NZ	New Zealand
RP	Received Pronunciation, see section 1.1
SA	South Africa(n)

Transcription systems for RP and GA are those used in the companion volume, McMahon (2002).

To readers

The title of this book, *International Varieties of English*, requires some comment. It might be expected that this would refer to varieties of English which are used internationally, but this is not its normal field of use. Instead, it is a well-established label for varieties of English which are used nationally in different places in the world. Although 'national varieties of English' might be a more transparent term, this widely accepted though slightly peculiar use of 'international varieties' is maintained in this book.

While most books on international varieties of English take each variety in turn and discuss the vocabulary, grammar and pronunciation which is special to that variety, this book aims to seek out generalities which determine the ways in which English will diverge in different locations. Accordingly, there are chapters dealing with matters such as vocabulary, grammar and pronunciation, but in each it is shown how the same fundamental principles apply to a number of different varieties with disparate outcomes. So the question is not *How do they speak English in X?* where 'X' is some Anglophone country, but rather *Why have the varieties of English round the world turned out the way they have?* Correspondingly, the exercises are designed to make students think about what it means to speak Australian or Falkland Islands English, what the historical influences on any given variety are, and how familiar notions such as 'standard' apply outside Britain or the USA.

I hope that this book will complement and be complemented by books which take a more traditional approach, and that this volume will be useful for courses which aim to consider the English language as used in a particular area or country as well as for courses which are intended to explore the linguistic principles underlying linguistic colonisation and globalisation.

Teachers and students alike are encouraged to go beyond the book by studying texts from various countries round the world, listening to speakers from these countries, and talking to them if at all possible. That, after all, is the best way to get a feel for how different the international Englishes can be, and how much they have in common.

Edinburgh Textbooks on the English Language

TITLES IN THE SERIES INCLUDE

An Introduction to English Syntax
Jim Miller

An Introduction to English Phonology
April McMahon

An Introduction to English Morphology
Andrew Carstairs-McCarthy

An Introduction to Middle English
Simon Horobin and Jeremy Smith

An Introduction to Old English
Richard Hogg

1 Background notions

This book is about the characteristics of the English language as it is used in various countries around the world. It is restricted, however, to those varieties of English spoken predominantly by native speakers of English. This means we will consider the kinds of English spoken in Britain, the USA, Canada, South Africa, Australia, New Zealand and the Falkland Islands, but will have little to say about the varieties spoken in Nigeria, Jamaica, Singapore, Hong Kong or the Philippines. This distinction will be spelt out in greater detail and justified further in section 2.2 and immediately below. Here I merely draw attention to this self-imposed limitation, and make the point that this book does not attempt to provide in-depth coverage of English in all the countries in which it has a significant place.

To some extent, this limitation is a consequence of the introductory nature of this text. The cases dealt with here are all the easy ones: they arise by putting speakers of different varieties of English together and letting a new variety emerge, influenced by surrounding languages in ways which will be explored in this book. These relatively simple processes also apply in more complex situations, but other factors also play important roles there. To deal with the situation in Nigeria or Singapore, we would need some understanding of the contact situation in which the varieties of English there developed, including the political and educational conditions. In particular we would need to know about the principles affecting languages in contact, especially where the language we are interested in remains a minority one for a long period. We would also have to know a lot more about the languages spoken in these areas at the time English was introduced – in both these cases, this means several languages. If we wanted to look at pidgin and creole languages such as Tok Pisin in Papua New Guinea or Krio in Sierra Leone we would need to know about the general principles which govern the process of simplification (producing pidgins) and the principles of reconstructing grammatical complexity (producing creoles). These are interesting issues, but not elementary ones.

The book is arranged as follows. In the rest of this chapter, some fundamental notions for the subject will be discussed. In Chapter 2 we will look at the spread of English, and ways of describing it. In subsequent chapters we will consider general problems concerned with the vocabulary, grammar, spelling and pronunciation of varieties of English around the world. We will see that the general sources of vocabulary, the types of variation in grammar, and so on, are remarkably similar, wherever the variety in question is spoken. In the last three chapters we look at the way colonial Englishes are affecting British English, trace the movement towards linguistic independence in the various countries being considered, and discuss the notion of standard in more detail.

This is not a book which will tell you all about Australian or Canadian English. There are many such works, starting with Trudgill and Hannah (1994; first published in 1982), and including papers in journals such as *World Englishes* and *English World-Wide*. There is even a series of books published as a companion series to the journal *English World-Wide*. These can give far more detailed information on the situation in each of the relevant countries and on the use of the linguistic structures which are found there. Instead, this book attempts to look for generalisations: the things which happen in the same way in country after country, and which would happen again in the same way if English speakers settled in numbers on some previously unknown island or on some new planet. This is done in the belief and the hope that descriptions of the individual varieties will be more meaningful if you understand how they got to be the way they are.

At the end of each chapter you will find some suggestions for further reading and some exercises. Answers to the exercises are provided in a section at the end of the book called 'Discussion of the exercises'. The exercises are intended to check and to extend your understanding of the material in the text, and to provide challenges for you to consider. They are not graded for difficulty, and vary considerably in the amount of time and effort they will require to complete, so take the advice of your teacher if you are in doubt as to which ones to attempt.

1.1 Accent, dialect, language and variety

You can usually tell after just a few words whether someone has a Scottish, Australian or American accent; you don't have to wait for them to say some particularly revealing local word or to use some special construction. The important thing about an accent is that it is something you hear: the accent you speak with concerns purely the sound you make when you talk, your pronunciation. Since everybody has a pronunciation of their language, everybody has an accent. Those people who say that somebody 'doesn't have an accent' either mean that the person concerned sounds just like they do themselves, or means that the accent used is the expected one for standard speakers to use. In either case, there is an accent. The accent in which Southern Standard British English is typically spoken, sometimes called 'BBC English', is usually termed 'Received Pronunciation' or 'RP' by linguists. That label will be used here in preference to McMahon's (2002) 'SSBE'.

What you speak with your accent is your individual version of a dialect – a kind of language which identifies you as belonging to a particular group of people. Again, everybody speaks one or more dialects. Standard Southern British English dialect is just one dialect among many. To recognise that this is true, you only have to think of that dialect from an international perspective: it marks the speaker as coming from a particular place (the south of England or perhaps just England) which is just one of the very many places where English is spoken. A dialect is made up of vocabulary items (what Carstairs-McCarthy 2002: 13 calls 'lexical items', that is words, approximately) and grammatical patterns, and is usually spoken with a particular accent, though in principle the accent may be divorced from the dialect (as when an American, in an attempt to mimic the English, calls someone 'old chap', but still sounds American).

Next we need to ask what the relationship is between the dialects of English and the language English. Unfortunately, linguists find it extremely difficult to answer this question. As far as the linguist is concerned, a language exists if people use it. If nobody ever used it, it would not exist. So if we say that *survey* is a word of English, we mean that people avail themselves of that word when they claim to be speaking English; and if we say that *scrurb* is, as far as we know, not a word of English we mean that, to the best of our knowledge, people claiming to speak English do not use this word at all. These judgements are based on what speakers of English do, not determined by some impersonal static authority. If we say 'The English language does not contain the word *scrurb*', this is just shorthand for 'people who claim to speak English do not use the word *scrurb*'. If we say '*scrurb* is not in the dictionary' we mean that lexicographers have not been aware of any speakers using this word as part of English. This shows that we cannot define a language independent of its speakers, but as we have seen, any one individual speaker speaks one particular dialect of a language. Thus this does not enable us to establish the relationship between a dialect (of English) and the language (English).

Now, it is clear that while all people who say they are speaking English have some features which they share, there are also ways in which they differ. Then we face the difficult question of whether they speak the same language or not (see further in section 8.5). It is probably true in one sense that nobody speaks exactly the same language as anybody else, but it is not very helpful to define a language in this way. (Some linguists use the term 'idiolect' for the language spoken by an individual.) But there is no simple way to decide how different two speakers can be and still be said to speak the same language. Mutual comprehensibility is often suggested as a criterion: if two speakers can understand each other they speak the same language. But this does not correspond to the way in which we normally use the word 'language'. Danish, Swedish and Norwegian speakers may be able to understand each other when they speak their own languages, but we usually regard Danish, Swedish and Norwegian as different languages. On the other hand, people from different parts of Britain or the USA may have great difficulty in understanding each other, yet we still say they are speaking the same language. There is a political element in the definition of a language.

To make matters worse, terms like *language* and *dialect* are terms which often carry a number of meanings in everyday usage which they do not have for the linguist. The warning *Watch your language!* or, for some people, just *Language!*, can be used tell someone to speak (more) politely, and the word *dialect* contains a number of potential traps for the unwary. *Dialect* may be understood as referring only to rural speech; it may be understood as referring only to non-standard language; it may be interpreted as implying 'quaint' or 'colourful' or 'unusual'; none of these are things which a linguist would necessarily wish to imply by using the word. Because the terms *dialect* and *language* are so difficult to define and so open to misinterpretation, it is often better to avoid them where possible.

To do this, we use the term 'variety'. We can use 'variety' to mean a language, a dialect, an idiolect or an accent; it is a term which encompasses all of these. The term 'variety' is an academic term used for any kind of language production, whether we are viewing it as being determined by region, by gender, by social class, by age or by our own inimitable individual characteristics. It will be frequently used in this book as a neutral term.

1.2 Home and colony

In Australia and New Zealand, the word 'home' (frequently with a capital <H> in writing) was, until very recently, used to refer to Britain, even by people who had been born in the colony and grown up without ever setting foot in Britain. In South Africa this use of 'home' died out rather earlier, as it did in the USA, though *The Oxford English Dictionary* shows the same usage in North America in the eighteenth century. No doubt a similar usage was found among the planters in Ireland. Such a usage is now mocked by young Australians and New Zealanders, but reflected a very important psychological state for many of the people involved.

If Britain was 'home', what was the other side of the coin? I shall here use the term 'colony' and its derivatives to contrast with 'home', even if the political entities thus denominated were at various times styled dominions, commonwealths or independent countries (such as the USA). The label is meant to be inclusive and general, and to capture what the various settlements have in common.

1.3 Colonial lag

One of the popular myths about the English language is that somewhere people are still speaking the kind of English that Chaucer or Shakespeare or Milton spoke. People were said to speak Chaucerian English in sixteenth-century Ireland (Görlach 1987: 91), and to this day are said to speak Shakespearian English in parts of the United States such as North Carolina and the Appalachians (Montgomery 1998). This myth does, of course, have some foundation in fact, though the mythical versions repeated above are gross exaggerations. The relevant fact is that some regional dialects of English retain old forms which have disappeared from the standard form of the language. *Holp* for the modern *helped* is one of the examples of 'Shakespearian' English that is regularly cited in the USA. The Australasian use of *footpath* for British *pavement* or American *sidewalk* was current in Britain when Australia and New Zealand were settled, and *pavement* is a more recent innovation (in that sense) in Britain. (The first citation showing the relevant meaning of *pavement* in *The Oxford English Dictionary* is from 1874.)

This conservatism in colonial varieties is, rather unfortunately, termed 'colonial lag' – unfortunately because the term gives the impression that the colonial variety will (or should) one day catch up with the home variety, though this is unlikely ever to happen. Colonial lag is a potential factor in distinguishing colonial varieties from their home counterparts in all levels of language: phonology, morphology, syntax, semantics and lexis. For instance, American English has never changed the length of the open front vowel before /f/, /θ/ and /s/ in words like *laugh*, *bath* and *castle*, which are accordingly pronounced /læf/, /bæθ/ and /kæsl/ in the USA with a phonologically short vowel, but with a phonologically long vowel in RP, South African English and New Zealand English (RP /lɑːf/, /bɑːθ/ and /kɑːsl/). American English has retained *gotten* while it has changed to *got* in standard varieties of British English (though there are some signs of a revival of *gotten* under the influence of the USA). In syntax, we may consider the so-called mandative subjunctive, illustrated in (1) below. This involves the use of an unmarked or stem-form verb with a third person singular after certain expressions of, for example, desire or obligation.

> (1) If the King Street commissars were not so invincibly stupid, they would have *insisted* that the movement *be* left severely alone (1964; cited from the *OED* and Denison 1998: 262).

This usage has remained in the US, while in British English there has been a tendency (one which may now be weakening, particularly in documents written in 'officialese') to prefer the construction with *should* in (1′).

> (1′) If the King Street commissars were not so invincibly stupid, they would have *insisted* that the movement *should be* left severely alone.

The example of *pavement* cited above shows semantic change in Britain that was not matched in Australia and New Zealand. Lexical lag can be illustrated with the word *bioscope*, until recently the word for 'cinema' in South Africa, long after the word had vanished in Britain. All these examples make the point that colonial lag can indeed be observed.

On the other hand, it is a lot easier to find examples of colonial innovation and British conservatism. The merger of unstressed /ə/ and /ɪ/ in Australian and New Zealand English leading to the homophony of pairs like *villagers* and *villages*, the preference for *dreamed* over *dreamt* in the USA, the re-invention of a second person plural *y'all, you guys, yous,* etc. in various parts of the world, the use of words for British flora and fauna for new species in the colonies and the invention of new terms all indicate the power of colonial innovation and home lag. So the question becomes, not whether there is any colonial lag, but how important a factor in the development of colonial Englishes colonial lag is, and whether it is more powerful in some areas than in others. This type of question should be borne in mind while reading the rest of the book.

1.4 Dialect mixing

It is well known that dialects differ in terms of a number of individual phonological, grammatical and lexical features. Such distinctions are typically drawn on maps as isoglosses, imaginary lines between two areas each of which has a uniform pronunciation, or grammatical or lexical usage, but which are distinct with relation to the particular feature under discussion.

For example, pouring boiling water on to tea-leaves to make tea goes by various names in different parts of England. The standard word is *brew*, and this is replacing an older *mash*, which in the 1950s could still be heard in Westmoreland, Yorkshire, Nottinghamshire, Derbyshire, Leicestershire, Northamptonshire, Warwickshire and most of Lincolnshire, as well as in some of the adjacent counties (Orton *et al.* 1978: Map L42). However, if we look at the forms found in Norfolk and Suffolk, which fall on the border between *brew* and *mash*, we find localities where both *brew* and *mash* are used, localities where both *draw* and *mash* are used, localities where both *make* and *mash* are used, and occasional localities where just *make* or just *scald* are used. There are a number of points to make about such data. First, it is mainly the case that we find standard *brew* in the *mash* areas rather than the other way round: *brew* is expanding at the expense of the older, non-standard form. Second, it is clear that at the border we find people choosing (possibly fairly randomly) between two forms, both of which are available to them. Third, sometimes people react to this excess of words by using neither, but bringing in another (*make, scald*) and thus cutting the Gordian knot. In any case, a single line on the map represents a great oversimplification of what is happening linguistically. On the ground we find speakers adapting their speech to the speech of their interlocutors, making choices to align themselves socially with one group or another, and using varieties which are not necessarily consistent. This situation is called 'dialect mixing'.

The same is true if we look at pronunciation rather than lexis. In the north of England, the word *chaff* is usually pronounced with a short vowel: [tʃaf]; in the south-east it is usually pronounced with a long back vowel: [tʃɑːf]. Between the two there is quite a large area where it is pronounced with a vowel which has the quality of the northern one, but the length of the southern one: [tʃaːf]. And where the [tʃaf] area meets the [tʃaːf] area we find pronunciations like [tʃæf], [tʃæːf] and [tʃɑːf] (Orton *et al.* 1978: Map Ph3). These represent both compromises and attempts to adopt the standard pronunciation to avoid the issue.

While such borders may move, they may also remain static for very long periods, with speakers at the boundaries speaking a mixed dialect which displays features of the dialects on either side.

You can feel the pull of the same forces every time you speak to someone whose variety of English is not the same as yours. If you are English and talk to an American, a Scot or an Australian, if you are American and find yourself talking to a Southerner or a New Yorker, if you are an Australian and you find yourself talking to someone from England or South Africa, you will probably notice that your English changes to accommodate to the English of the person you are talking to. This can even happen when you don't particularly like the person you are talking to, or where you have bad associations with the kind of English they speak. You may or may not be aware that you are doing this, and you will probably be unaware that your interlocutor is doing it as well, but the modifications will occur.

Such changes are difficult enough to describe when just two dialects come in contact with each other or when just two speakers come face to face. Typically, in the colonial situation, a lot of speakers of many different dialects come face to face, and in the short term the result is a period of diversity where everyone is accommodating to everyone else. During this period, speakers may not be aware of any trends or emerging patterns. Gradually, however, order emerges from the chaos, the trends become clearer and a new mixed dialect is formed. This mixed dialect will have some of the features of the various dialects which have gone into making it up.

But which features will it have? Is it predictable from the input dialects which forms will persist, and is it deducible from the new mixed dialect where the forms have come from? These questions have been considered in some detail for a number of years now, and no absolute consensus has yet emerged. But perhaps the simplest hypothesis is that in most cases the form used by the majority will be the form that survives in the new mixed dialect (Trudgill *et al.* 2000). There are other factors which appear to be relevant: pronunciations which are stigmatised as being particularly regional (such as making *lush* rhyme with *bush*, or making *sap* and *zap* sound the same) do not appear to survive in the colonies. Such a factor may be no more than a generalisation of the simplest hypothesis, though: if something is strictly regional in Britain, fewer people who use this feature are likely to be part of the mix in the colony, and thus the feature is unlikely to survive. Another suggestion, given the label of 'swamping' by Lass (1990), is that where variability is present (for example between /lʌʃ/ and /lʊʃ/ for *lush*), the variant which is in use in the south-east of England – taken to be the variety with the highest prestige – will always win out. However, there is growing evidence that it is not always the variant from the south-east of England which emerges victorious in the colonies (see Bauer 1999 on New Zealand English), and it may be that where the non-south-eastern variants win out it is because they are used by a majority of speakers.

Perhaps the most difficult feature of pronunciation to deal with in this context is the fate of non-prevocalic /r/ in words like *shore* and *cart*. All varieties of English retain an /r/ sound of some type in words like *red* and *roof,* but in *shore* and *cart* where there was once an /r/ before something which is not a vowel (either a pause or a consonant), there is no /r/ in the standard English of England, though the older pronunciation with /r/ is not only reflected in the spelling, but heard in many regional dialects from Reading to Blackburn. Varieties which retain the historical /r/ are sometimes referred to as 'rhotic' varieties or (particularly in American texts) 'r-ful' varieties; those which do not retain it are called 'non-rhotic' or 'r-less' varieties. The non-rhotic pattern did not become part of standard English pronunciation in England until the eighteenth century, but traces of it can be found in the sixteenth (Dobson 1968: 914).

Precisely how rhoticity and non-rhoticity spread into North America is a very complex matter. According to Crystal (1988: 224; 1995: 93) the first settlers in Massachusetts were from eastern counties of England, and rhoticity was already disappearing from there at the time of settlement in 1620. New England, including Massachusetts, remains non-rhotic to this day, with Boston speech being caricatured with the expression *Hahvahd Yahd* for *Harvard Yard.* Settlers in Virginia, on the other hand, were mainly from the west of England, and took their non-prevocalic /r/s with them to a new continent, and their version of English (in this regard) spread westward across America. While this version of events has a pleasing simplicity, it cannot be the entire story, if only because Jamestown, Virginia, the site of the first settlement in what is now the USA, is in the heart of a traditionally non-rhotic area. It is the people who settled slightly later who must have provided the basically rhotic population. We need to consider at least two other factors. The first is that the major ports along the eastern seaboard remained in constant contact with England, and could thus be affected by changes in English norms. The second is the large number of Scots–Irish immigrants who arrived in the early eighteenth century – perhaps a quarter of a million of them in a fifty-year period. These people spoke a rhotic variety of English.

Most of this gives the expected pattern. Speakers in Massachusetts were originally non-rhotic because the majority of the immigrants were non-rhotic. North America as a whole became mainly rhotic because most of the English-speaking settlers were rhotic. The case of Jamestown itself is not necessarily as complex as it seems: of the 105 settlers (all men) on the original ship which landed in 1607, only thirty-eight were still alive eight months later (Bridenbaugh 1980: 119), so that the settlers who must have influenced the pronunciation of the colony must have been later arrivals, perhaps even eighteenth-century arrivals. It is certain that factors other than the origins of the first settlers played a role. Whatever the contribution of maritime contacts with England in the late seventeenth century, we can see a much more recent example of external norms having an effect: although New York City was traditionally non-rhotic, it became the prestige norm to pronounce non-prevocalic /r/ there in the course of the twentieth century due to the influence of the mainstream US rhoticity.

Similarly, it is no great surprise to find that Australian English is non-rhotic. While large numbers of Irish and Scots did settle in Australia, in 1861 the English-born people in Australia outnumbered the Irish by more than two to one, and the number of English-born living there was greater than the number of Irish, Scottish, US and Canadian-born people combined.

The situation in New Zealand is far less clear-cut. In 1881, there were nearly as many settlers born in Scotland and Ireland as there were settlers born in England, but the difference was not great, and many of the English settlers would have spoken a rhotic variety. To get some idea, we can look at the number of immigrants in 1874 (see Table 1.1, data from McKinnon *et al.* 1997). Note that if even a quarter of the immigrants from some of the vaguely defined areas (such as 'Rest of England') were rhotic, the number of rhotic immigrants would have been greater than the number of non-rhotic ones. These figures do not take into account the destinations of the individual speakers in New Zealand: if all the rhotic speakers ended up in one place and all the non-rhotic speakers in another, we would expect this to lead to two distinct dialect areas. Things are not as clear as that. We do have some evidence that the South Island of New Zealand was largely rhotic in the 1880s, although the same was not true of the North Island at that time. Today rhoticity is confined to part of the southern end of the South Island. If we are to stay with a 'majority rules' view of the fate of /r/ in New Zealand we must either assume that the majority is influenced by continuing immigration – so that something which was once a majority form can, because of continued immigration, become a minority form – or we must assume that the majority is determined over quite a large community, not just the immediately local community. Either hypothesis causes problems in the New Zealand context because of the retention of rhoticity in one small area of the country.

In New Zealand, therefore, a simple rule of majority among the early settlers may not be sufficient to explain everything about the pronunciation of the mixed dialect used there. We may also have to consider factors such as subsequent immigration patterns, the geographic isolation of particular groups of speakers, and where particular groups of

Table 1.1 Sources of immigration to New Zealand in 1874, showing
probable rhoticity of immigrants

Rhotic		Non-rhotic	
Origin	Number	Origin	Number
Lanarkshire	774	Essex, Middlesex (including London)	1,566
Ulster	1,189	Channel Islands	291
Cork and Kerry	912	Hampshire, Surrey, Sussex, Kent (note: not all non-rhotic)	1,973
Elsewhere in Ireland	1,670	Rest of England, Scotland and Wales (note: not all non-rhotic)	4,425
Warwick, Gloucester, Oxford	1,188		
Devon and Cornwall	1,055		
Shetland	262		
Total	**7,050**	**Total**	**8,255**

speakers see the prestige variety as coming from (in the New Zealand
context, speakers in rhotic areas may have seen Scotland as a centre of
prestige; in the New York context, the prestige comes from the broadcast
standard in the USA). Overall we can predict a great deal about the form
of a colonial mixed dialect from the form used by the majority of the
settlers, but it is not yet clear how large the remaining gaps are. It would
be unwise yet to assume that the majority explains everything, though it
certainly explains a lot.

Exercises

1. Choose any three features from any colonial varieties of English,
and decide whether they illustrate colonial lag or not. For instance, you
might choose the Canadian 'raised' pronunciation of words like *out* and
house, which have a noticeably different vowel from that in *loud* or *browse*,
the American use of *Did you eat yet?* rather than *Have you eaten (yet)?*, and
the American use of *biscuit* for something which is not sweet, but in principle any three features will do. Reflect on how you decide in each case.

2. Record yourself having independent conversations with two people,
each of whom speaks a different variety of English. Can you hear differences in your pronunciation in the two cases? If so, what have you

changed? If not, what might be preventing change? If you cannot set this up, try recording a single interviewer in the broadcast media interviewing two different people who speak different kinds of English, and ask the same questions about the interviewer.

3. The following brief passage is taken from R. D. Blackmore's *Lorna Doone* (1869, chapter 3). The author is trying to represent the local Devon speech of his character. Which non-standard features in the text show accent, and which show dialect?

> Never God made vog as could stop their eysen ... Zober, lad, goo zober now, if thee wish to see thy moother.

4. Note that in New York it is now overtly prestigious to have a rhotic pronunciation, while non-rhotic pronunciations are also found, but have less prestige. Both rhotic and non-rhotic pronunciations are also found side-by-side in parts of England like Reading, Bath and Blackburn. Which pronunciation is seen as more prestigious in these places: the rhotic or the non-rhotic? Why? What does this say about standards in general?

Recommendations for reading

Görlach (1987) is a good source on colonial lag. While Görlach himself is sceptical, he cites sources which have given the idea a warmer welcome. The origin of the term 'colonial lag' is obscure to me.

The main source on dialect mixing is Trudgill (1986), as updated by Trudgill *et al.* (2000).

For a helpful discussion of the establishment of rhoticity in the USA, and the Jamestown settlement in particular, see Wolfram and Schilling-Estes (1998: 94–9).

2 English becomes a world language

2.1 The spread of English

At the time of Elizabeth I (1533–1603), there were at most seven million native speakers of English. There were very few non-native speakers of English. Even Richard Mulcaster, an enthusiastic supporter of the English language, and the headmaster of the school attended by the poet Edmund Spenser, admitted in 1582 that 'our English tung ... is of small reatch, it stretcheth no further then this Iland of ours, naie not there ouer all' (quoted from Görlach 1991: 229–30). Dutch was seen as a more useful language to learn than English. Yet by the time of Elizabeth II (1926–) the number of native speakers of English had increased to some 350 million. If we add non-native speakers to the total, we can double that number.

This huge expansion cannot be attributed to any great merit in the English language as such. Rather it must be attributed to historical developments, many of them accidental, by which England (and later Britain) gained a huge empire and then Britain and its former colonies gained influence far beyond the boundaries of that empire.

Even by the time that Elizabeth I came to the throne of England, the spread of English had started. An English-speaking area had been established round Dublin in Ireland, within what was called the Pale. Beyond the Pale there was (from the English viewpoint) no civilisation. The Pale was established by the Normans in the twelfth century, but it persisted, varying in size, until the seventeenth century. Another sign of expansionism was the exploration of Canada by the Cabots in the final years of the fifteenth century, laying the foundation for English claims to Canada.

The first years of Elizabeth I's reign saw further expansionist moves. Although there had been Norman settlements in Wales, and an English Prince of Wales since 1301, the Statute of Wales in 1535 imposed English as the official language of the country for all legal purposes, and prevented Welsh speakers from holding office unless they used English

13

for official purposes. This was only feasible because there had been an unlegislated imposition of English in the two preceding centuries, with settlements of English-speaking people in Wales, and trade being carried out mainly in English.

By 1553, English ships were trading with West Africa (present-day Nigeria), and the slave trade started some ten years later. In the 1580s the first English settlements were made in North America, in Canada in 1583 and at Roanoke in present-day North Carolina in 1584. The Roanoke settlement remains a puzzle to this day. Although we know that the first English child to be born in North America was born there (and named Virginia in honour of Queen Elizabeth), all the settlers mysteriously disappeared and could not be found when English ships returned – much later than expected – with provisions.

In 1603, with the death of Elizabeth I, James VI of Scotland also became James I of England, and Scotland and England were merged politically into Great Britain. This had the effect of spreading English influence into Scotland, especially through the use of the King James version of the Bible, published in 1611.

The year 1607 was a fateful one for the English language. The first lasting settlement in North America was established at Jamestown in Virginia. The settlers who formed the permanent population in this area were largely from the English west country, and traces of their varieties of English can still be found in North American English generally and in the eastern seaboard dialects of Virginia in particular.

The other major event at this time was the plantation of Ulster. Settlements (or plantations) of Englishmen had been tried by Elizabeth as a way of quelling rebellion in Ireland and securing the English, Protestant, throne against the Catholic Irish. James I continued the policy, confiscating lands of Irish nobility who were deemed to have rebelled against English rule, and selling them to English and Scottish settlers who had to fulfil certain criteria, one of which was (in effect) being Protestant. Although it took a long time for the plantations to have the desired effect, the commonalities between the speech of Northern Ireland and western Lowland Scotland today stem largely from the number of Scots who settled in Ulster from 1607 onwards.

The next major settlement in North America took place in 1620, when the *Mayflower*, carrying people from the eastern counties of England, failed to reach Virginia and landed instead in present-day Massachusetts, where they founded the town of Plymouth. As pointed out in section 1.4, this was a non-rhotic settlement, and the area remains non-rhotic to this day.

At about the same time, in 1621, a charter was granted for a Scottish settlement in Nova Scotia, but there was not enough money to pursue the project, and Nova Scotia remained little more than a name on a map for some time after that as far as the British were concerned.

We pass quickly over the next hundred years, during which time the British hold on Ireland was strengthened, and the settlement of eastern North America continued.

In 1763, Canada was ceded to the British by the French. 'Canada' then referred only to the French-speaking areas, not the large country we know today, which was not to be established for another hundred years. From our point of view this was an important step because it allowed a British foothold in North America to be maintained after the American Declaration of Independence in 1776. The British did not recognise the United States of America until 1783, when disappointed loyalists fled into Canada.

By this time, Captain James Cook had mapped the coastline of New Zealand (1769) and met his first kangaroo (1770). He claimed both Australia and New Zealand for the British crown, though it was not until 1788 that the first penal colony was established at Botany Bay (present-day Sydney). That was just a few years before the occupation of the South African Cape Colony in 1795.

So by the opening of the nineteenth century, English had spread to every corner of the world, and in the course of the nineteenth and twentieth centuries the number of speakers of the language, and the language's own prestige, grew and grew. In 1800 the population of the United States was about 5.3 million; by 1900 it had grown to 76 million. By the close of the twentieth century it was heading for 250 million. The growth was achieved by spreading out to cover more land, and by accepting immigrants from elsewhere in the world. In 1803 Louisiana (a much larger area than the current state) was bought from the French; in 1819 Florida was bought from Spain; and all Zorro fans know the story of the California purchase! Many of the immigrants came from the British Isles as a result of the agricultural reforms and other related events that were going on there.

As early as the time of Elizabeth I, agricultural practice was changing in England, with tracts of land under cultivation being made larger for greater economy. For the landowners to get these large tracts of land, the poor were thrown out of their homes and off the land. This led to a gradual deruralisation of the British populace and a move to the cities, which accelerated with the arrival of the industrial revolution and the need for factory workers.

Although this trend is visible at least until the end of the nineteenth century, there are two major events which had an effect on the kinds of emigrants from the British Isles who took their English out into the world. The first was the Highland Clearances, following on from the failure of the second Jacobite rebellion in 1745, as a result of which English had been imposed in much of the Highlands. The population of the area was growing faster than the capacity of the land to feed the people. The two factors of population growth and reduced access to land for crops forced people to emigrate. The same was true in Ireland, whose population in 1841 was over eight million, making it the most densely populated country in Europe at the time. In both countries the small-holders were hindering the emergence of large profitable estates, and were being moved off the land. Then in 1845 came the potato famine. This hit hardest in Ireland, where between half a million and a million people died (more often of disease brought on by weakness than of actual starvation) in a four-year period. Although the potato was not such an important part of the diet in England and Scotland, it again meant that the land could not carry the population. The twin pressures of lack of food and landowners trying to gain greater incomes from their land meant that emigration was the only alternative to starvation for many people.

The population of Ireland has never recovered. It fell by two million in ten years. In the course of the nineteenth century nearly five million Irish people emigrated to the United States alone (McCrum *et al.* 1986: 188), and that doesn't take any account of those who ended up in Canada, Australia and New Zealand. Into the late nineteenth century emigrants from the British Isles to Canada, the United States, Australia and New Zealand were being driven by the same motivation of lack of land and opportunity.

A summary of the expansion of English until the mid-nineteenth century is presented in Table 2.1.

Although this explains how English speakers spread around the world, it does not tell us much about the great political power that has accompanied that spread. The political power grew not only from the number of countries where English-speaking people settled, but from the economic and military strength of those people.

This started in the reign of Elizabeth I, with explorers going out to seek new trade. This was a deliberate policy for Elizabeth, who had inherited a virtually bankrupt nation which became rich during her reign. Although the policy did not keep all subsequent monarchs affluent (James I sold off bits of Ireland partly to help fill his coffers), most of Britain's wealth came through its trade coupled, in the nineteenth century, with its industrial strength. At the same time there was a feeling of moral superiority, which gave rise to political and religious

Table 2.1 The expansion of English

Date	Britain	North America	Africa	Australasia
c.550	English in Lowland Scotland			
1066	Norman invasion of England; some English flee to Scotland			
1169	Norman settlement in south-east Ireland			
1172	The English king becomes Lord of Ireland			
1301	First Prince of Wales			
1497		Cabot reaches Newfoundland		
1536, 1542	Act of Union with Wales			
1553			Trade with WestAfrica	
1584		Roanoke settlement		
1607	Plantations of Ulster	Jamestown settlement		
1611	King James version of the Bible published			
1620		Plymouth settlement		
1642				Tasman discovers Tasmania and New Zealand
1650	Cromwellian settlements in Ireland			
1707	Act of Union with Scotland			
1745	Highland Clearances			

Table 2.1 The expansion of English *continued*

Date	Britain	North America	Africa	Australasia
1763		Canada ceded to the British		
1769				Cook circumnavigates New Zealand
1770				Cook claims east Australia for the crown
1776		Declaration of Independence		
1788			Period of colonisation of West Africa	Botany Bay settlement
1795			Occupation of the Cape Colony	
1800	Act of Union with Ireland			
1840				Treaty of Waitangi: settlement of New Zealand
1845	Potato famine			

evangelicalism, and which allowed the colonisation of much of the world to proceed. The feeling that the British were right and that they were doing everyone a favour by bringing them democracy, bureaucracy, Christianity, literacy and the English language became extraordinarily well established. This unreflecting arrogance seems odd today, but was genuinely felt in the colonial period. It leaves its traces in the reluctance of English-speakers to learn other languages, among other things.

In its turn, US power has been based on industrial and military muscle. From the time the US entered the First World War in 1917 right through to the present, the US has been one of the major military powers in the world.

The economic and military might has left behind it traders and soldiers who have had to learn English to do their job properly. Because industry, exploration and military demands needed and contributed to learning, much of scientific discourse came to be carried out primarily in English, especially in the second half of the twentieth century. It is the combination of industry, trade, war and learning all of which use English that has put English in its position as the world's pre-eminent language. And while Britain and the US have driven that combination of factors, the other countries under discussion here have benefitted from the fact that those two have made English so important.

2.2 Models of English

In textbooks you may well have seen family trees for the Indo-European languages in which English, German, Dutch and Friesian are daughters of a West Germanic proto-language. This, along with a proto-North Germanic language and Gothic, is one of the daughters of a Common Germanic language (see Figure 2.1). Each of the daughter languages is a descendant of its mother (which may or may not actually be an attested language, and if attested, may or may not still exist), deriving from it by a series of linguistic changes which distinguish it from its sisters. The family tree model (not always presented vertically on the page as in Figure 2.1) is one simple model of the ways in which languages are related each other. This model can also be applied to the diversity of English, which we can then, perhaps, term 'Englishes'. Lass (1987: 274) terms the overseas (including North American) varieties of English 'extra-territorial Englishes' or ETEs.

The model in Figure 2.1 presents a very simplified outline of the development of one language from another. It might seem at first glance that we could draw a parallel diagram to show the development of varieties of English. If we say that Canadian English has developed from US English, and that New Zealand English has developed from Australian English, we could represent this in a family tree like the partial one in Figure 2.2.

The difficulty with this simple model is that it does not provide a way to represent the influence that the Englishes spoken in Scotland and Ireland have had on North American Englishes, or to represent the double source of Canadian English in English and US Englishes. Of course, the same was true in Figure 2.1, where the influence of Low German and that of modern English on Danish are not represented. This lack is just more obvious when we are closer to the varieties concerned, and when we are considering relatively short time-spans.

The implication of this model is that English is beginning to split up into a number of daughter languages, in the way that Latin once split up into, for example, Italian, French, Spanish and Portuguese. There is some evidence to support this point of view, which is becoming well-established in the linguistic discussions about English (see McArthur

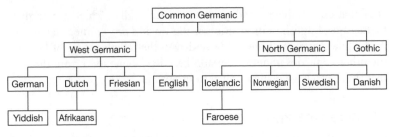

Figure 2.1 The Germanic languages

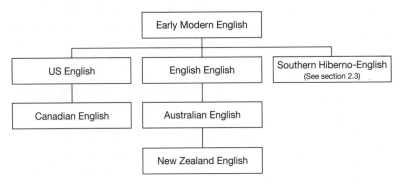

Figure 2.2 Hypothetical partial family tree for Englishes

1998 for ample evidence). If this model is accurate, we would expect the various kinds of English to become less like each other with time, and to end up becoming mutually unintelligible. Anyone who has heard a broad Tyneside speaker from England and a broad Texan speaker from the US trying to talk to each other might believe this era is already upon us. We will return to just how valid this picture of the development of English is in section 8.5.

An alternative model is presented by Görlach (1990a: 42), and can be seen in Figure 2.3. Görlach's model goes from the most widespread variety of English (in the centre) to the most local varieties (round the rim). A rather similar model is presented by McArthur (1987; see Figure 2.4) with the difference that the hub of the circle is seen as being a standard (something which Görlach 1990a: 42 specifically denies), and that McArthur includes creoles like Tok Pisin on a par with other regional varieties, while Görlach puts them on a different stratum. These models do not show origins and influences, but view English as a set of differing standards (each of which has the potential to develop into a different language), held together by the common heritage of world English at the

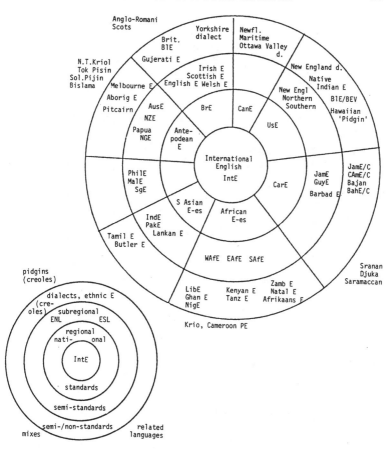

Figure 2.3 Görlach's model of Englishes

hub. These images fail to show that two very different types of English are involved: varieties spoken primarily by native speakers of English and varieties originally spoken by second-language learners of English. In the one case speakers have emigrated to countries taking their language with them; in the other, English has displaced another fully functional language or set of languages.

This division is taken up in a model by Kachru (1985), shown in Figure 2.5. The 'inner circle' of English is made up of those countries where English is a native language, the 'outer circle' of those where English is a post-colonial second language (frequently with many speakers whose dominant and perhaps only language is English), and the 'expanding circle' is made up of those countries where English is a foreign language.

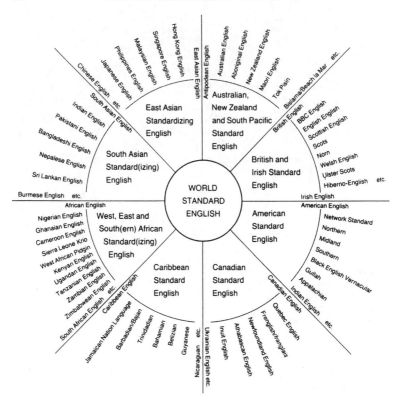

Figure 2.4 McArthur's model of Englishes

The difference may be viewed in terms of the number of domains in which English is used: in the 'inner circle' English is used in all domains, in the 'outer circle' it is frequently used in education (particularly in advanced education) and administration, in the 'expanding circle' it is used mostly in trade and international interaction.

There are, however, some problems with the view presented in Figure 2.5 as well. It is not clear how much is intended to be included under 'UK', or where the English of Ireland is supposed to fit into the general picture. South Africa, with over three million first-language speakers of English, is notably missing from the figure.

The reasons for the distinction between the three circles are worth considering. The expanding circle contains countries where English is used as a foreign language, but the native/foreign language distinction will not help us draw the line between the inner and outer circles: these days there are many people in countries like India and Singapore whose

Inner circle:
Australia
Canada
New Zealand
UK
USA

Outer circle:
Bangladesh
Ghana
India
Kenya
Malaysia
Nigeria
Pakistan
Philippines
Singapore
Sri Lanka

Expanding circle:
China
Egypt
Indonesia
Israel
Japan
Korea
Nepal
Saudi Arabia
Taiwan
USSR
Zimbabwe

Figure 2.5 Kachru's concentric circles of English

only language is English – and it is for this reason that Lass' 'mother-tongue ETEs' for the inner circle varieties does not seem like a good label. Rather the distinction is in the way in which the English language came to be important in the relevant countries.

First we must see England (if not the whole UK) as different from other places on the chart: English developed naturally there as the language of the people. While it has been strongly affected by various invasions, English is endemic in England. Everywhere else, English has been introduced. In the inner circle countries except the UK, a large group of English-speaking people arrived bringing their language with them, and they became a dominant population group in the new environment. Although local populations eventually had to learn English too, they were outnumbered by those for whom English was the major (in many cases the only) means of communication. In outer circle countries, by contrast, the local population for whom English was a foreign language were the dominant group, and the English language was imposed on them for the purposes of administration, trade, religion and education. The result was that even when people in these countries adopted English, it was an English strongly influenced by the local languages, whose direct descent from the English of England had been broken. We can summarise this neatly (and only slightly inaccurately) by saying that the inner circle represents places to which people were exported and the outer circle the places to which the language was exported.

However, national varieties of English within the UK do not fit neatly with this binary division. In much of Wales it was the language which was imposed (though there was also some movement of population). In Ireland, too, there was a mixture of types: on the one hand the plantations involved the importation of English by the importation of English speakers, on the other, many of the distinctive points of Irish English (see section 2.3) arise from contamination from the Irish language, which is typically the situation in places where English is a second language. The same is true in Scotland, although there we have the extra complication of Scots, which will be discussed in section 2.3. We might, therefore, see all these varieties as belonging to the outer circle. At the same time, English has been established in these countries for so long, and has been so clearly influenced by the language of England, that these countries have varieties of English which behave more like inner circle varieties than like outer circle varieties.

There is an extra point to be considered with the Englishes spoken in Ireland and Scotland: They have provided so much of the input to New World and southern hemisphere varieties of English, it is perhaps more useful from the point of view of this book to view them as part of the colonising drift from the British Isles than as among the first of the colonised.

South Africa presents a difficult case in terms of Figure 2.5 (as is admitted by Kachru 1985: 14). Although English was carried to the Cape by speakers from England in the early nineteenth century, the majority of users of English in South Africa today are speakers of English as a second language. Because there is a continuous history of English being used by some people across all domains, we can view South Africa as belonging peripherally to the inner circle, although there are many features of the outer circle.

This book is concerned with the Englishes used in the inner circle. More specifically, it is concerned with the relationship between the varieties of English used in the British Isles and those varieties used in former British colonies which now belong to Kachru's inner circle. Some of the problems that are raised by these inner circle varieties – questions of borrowing and substrate (a less dominant language or variety which influences the dominant one), for instance – are also problems shared by Englishes from the outer circle. However, inner circle varieties raise other questions too: can we locate a British origin for each variety, and how does the new variety emerge from the conflicting input dialects, for instance. Accordingly there are, despite the differences between the varieties, recurring issues and patterns which justify treating them as a set.

2.3 English in Scotland and Ireland

Having decided in section 2.2 not to treat the varieties of English in Scotland and Ireland as colonial varieties but as colonising ones, we could choose simply to ignore the complex linguistic situations in these countries, and treat each country as linguistically monolithic. Unfortunately, this is so far from the truth that it will not do even as a first approximation and a more nuanced approach is called for.

Let us begin with Scotland. Until the Highland Clearances, the people in the Highlands of Scotland were mainly Gaelic-speaking. Scottish Gaelic has been retreating in the face of some form of English ever since then, and is now mainly spoken in the Hebrides, and even there alongside English. Although Gaelic was once spoken in parts of the Lowlands as well, the people in most of the Lowlands of Scotland have spoken a Germanic language since at least the seventh century. Originally this Germanic language was used throughout Northumbria (the land between the Humber and the Firth of Forth), but before the Norman Conquest the northern part of Northumbria, as far south as the Tweed, had become part of Scotland, and this language became a dominant one in Scotland. By the time of James VI of Scotland (who became James I of England), the version of this language spoken in Scotland had become known as 'Scottis'. With the union of the crowns, Scottis fell more and more under the influence of English norms, but it survived as a vernacular language, and is today called Scots.

There is some discussion as to whether Scots is a dialect of English or a language in its own right (see McArthur 1998: 138–42). This is of no direct relevance in the present context (though see section 1.1 on the difficulty in defining a language). What is important is that many Scots have a range of varieties available to them, from Scots at the most local end of the scale to standard British English (at least in its written form) at the most formal end. While it is in theory possible to distinguish, for example, Scots /hem/ *hame* from English /hom/ *home* pronounced in a Scottish way, in practice it is no simple matter to draw a firm line between Scots and English. If we wish to call this entire range 'Scottish English', perhaps on the grounds that there is a Scottish standard of English, though not one explicitly set down (see Chapter 8), we must nevertheless recall that Scottish English is not uniform in pronunciation, grammar or vocabulary, and is sometimes more like the English of England, and sometimes more like Scots.

Although English was established in Ireland by the fourteenth century, there appears to have been a decline in its usage until the sixteenth century. By the time of Elizabeth I, the English did not expect the Irish – not even those of English descent – to speak English. While this seems to have been outsiders' misperception, there is evidence that English speakers in Ireland at the period were bilingual in English and Irish. Whatever the state of English in Ireland in the sixteenth century, there was a resurgence in its use in the seventeenth century when Cromwell settled English people there to counteract the Catholic influence. The English deriving from this settlement is now usually called 'Hiberno-English', or 'Southern Hiberno-English' to distinguish it from the language of the English settlers in Ulster. Meanwhile, Ulster had been 'planted' with some English, but mainly with Scots settlers under James I. The language of the Scots settlers is called 'Ulster-Scots', and the people are known as the 'Scots-Irish'. There were approximately 150,000 Scots settlers in Ulster, and about 20,000 English ones in the early seventeenth century (Adams 1977: 57). Although the Scots were much more numerous and the influence of their language on their English co-settlers persists to the present day, we can still find a Northern Hiberno-English in the areas which were English-dominated which is distinct from the Ulster-Scots.

Even if we are not going to treat the Englishes of Scotland and Ireland as colonial varieties as discussed in section 2.2, we need to know some things about these two varieties. Because of the number of emigrants from Scotland and Ireland, these varieties of English have had a surprisingly strong influence on the development of varieties outside the British Isles, often in ways which are not appreciated. While the varieties from Scotland and Ireland are often different, they also have much in common. There are at least two possible reasons for this. The first is that where there is substrate influence on English in these two cases it is from two closely related Celtic languages, Irish and Scottish Gaelic. Parallel influences are likely to have led to parallel developments, so we would expect similarities in the two varieties for that reason. It turns out, though, that most of the parallels of this type are in vocabulary. The second reason is the history of Ireland. We have seen that much of the plantation in Ulster was from Scotland in the seventeenth century, and that Ulster-Scots is a direct descendant of a Scottish variety of English. This common development means that similarities in the two varieties arise from their common source. Moreover, the two varieties did not have very long to drift apart before the emigration from Scotland and Ireland began.

This is not the place to give a full description of Irish and Scottish varieties of English. We can, however, point to a few phenomena which are relatively easily pinpointed as originating in one of the two, and which are found in other varieties round the world. Much of the Irish material here comes from Trudgill and Hannah (1994) and Filppula (1999).

2.3.1 Vocabulary

It is not possible to list all the words from the English of Scotland and Ireland that might occur in other varieties, or even give a core finding list. Here are some random examples of Scottish and Irish words which are found in other parts of the English-speaking world. Some of them may also be found in the northern part of England, but they are not part of standard English in England. Where some of these words are widespread or standard in countries outside Britain, they are almost certainly derived from Scottish and Irish: *messages* ('shopping'), *piece* ('sandwich, snack'), *pinkie* ('little finger'), *slater* ('woodlouse'), *stay* (additional meaning 'live'), *wee* ('small'), *youse* ('you, plural').

2.3.2 Grammar

- More generalised use of reflexive pronouns than in standard English English: *It was yourself said it.* (Hiberno-English)
- An indefinite anterior perfect without auxiliary *have*: *Were you ever in Dublin?* (Hiberno-English)
- The use of *after* as an immediate perfect: *He was only after getting the job* 'He had just got the job'. (Hiberno-English)
- The use of an included object with a perfect: *They hadn't each other seen for four years.* (Hiberno-English)
- The use of *be* as a perfect auxiliary with *go, come* and an ill-defined set of other verbs: *All the people are come down here.* (Hiberno-English)
- The use of inversion in indirect questions: *She asked my mother had she any cloth.* (Hiberno-English)
- The use of resumptive pronouns: *A man that the house was on his land.* (Scottish English, Hiberno-English, Ulster-Scots)

- The use of the past participle after *want*, *need* (this is sometimes seen as omission of *to be*, rather than as an alternative to a present participle): *This shirt needs washed.* After the same verbs, the use of directional particles: *The cat wants out.* (Scottish English, Ulster-Scots)
- A preference for *will* rather than *shall* in all positions. (Scottish English, Hiberno-English, Ulster-Scots)
- A tendency to leave *not* uncontracted: *Did you not?* rather than *Didn't you?* (Scottish English, Ulster-Scots)
- The use of *yet* with the simple past rather than the perfect: *Did you get it yet?* (Scottish English, Hiberno-English, Ulster-Scots)

2.3.3 Pronunciation

- Varieties of English in both Scotland and Ireland are rhotic (see section 1.4), although the quality of the /r/ is different in the two cases; both use a phoneme /x/ in a word like *loch/lough*, and both retain a distinction between *weather* and *whether*.
- The Scottish Vowel Length Rule is a complicated part of Scottish phonology whose description is not entirely agreed upon. What is clear is that one of its results is to make vowels longer when they are at the end of a stem than if they are immediately followed by a /d/ within the same stem. This means that *tied* (where the stem is *tie*) has a longer vowel than *tide*, and in this pair, the quality of the two vowels is usually also different. But there is the same length distinction, with no quality difference, in pairs like *brewed* and *brood*, which thus do not rhyme.
- In Hiberno-English there is an unrounded vowel in the LOT lexical set, so [lɑt] rather than [lɒt].
- /l/ is dark in all positions in Scottish English and clear in all positions in Irish varieties.
- In Scottish English there is final stress on *harass*, *realise* and initial stress in *frustrate*.
- In Scottish English the word *houses* is usually /haʊsɪz/.
- Southern Hiberno-English frequently replaces the dental fricatives in words like *thin* and *that* with dental plosives.

Exercises

1. Consider Figure 2.4. Look at any two sectors in the diagram and provide a critique of the figure as it stands.

2. Consider the two maps provided on pages 30–1, one showing the

places in the Atlantic states of the US where *bristle* is pronounced with [ʌ] in the first syllable (from Kurath and McDavid 1961: Map 59), and the other places in England where *bristle* was traditionally pronounced either with [ʌ] or with [ʊ] in the first syllable (based on Kolb *et al.* 1979: 162). How would you explain the distribution of this pronunciation of *bristle* in the USA?

3. In Figure 2.2 it is suggested that New Zealand English is a direct descendant of Australian English. What would the alternative be, and how would you expect to be able to test which alternative is the better way of drawing the tree?

Recommendations for reading

Crystal (1995; 1997: especially chapter 2) and McCrum *et al.* (1986) provide excellent coverage of the spread of English. Many histories of English cover the spread in some detail. A particularly interesting approach is given by Bailey (1991). Leith (1983) gives good coverage of the spread of English through Britain. The history of English in Ireland is summarised in Kallen (1997). For English in Scotland see McClure (1994).

The various models of English are discussed in some detail by Crystal (1995: 106–11) and McArthur (1998: chapter 4).

Map 1

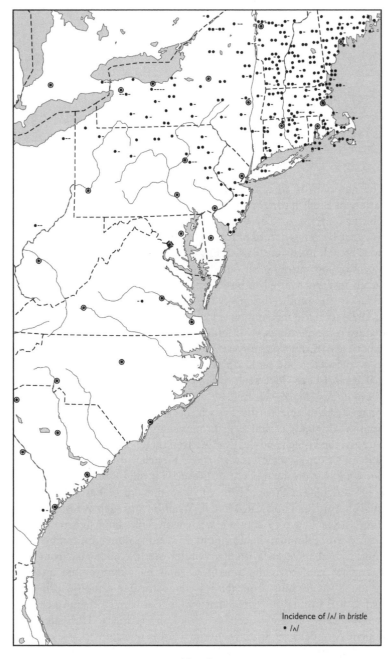

Incidence of /ʌ/ in *bristle*
• /ʌ/

Map 2

3 Vocabulary

The question of what is included in the vocabulary of a particular variety of English (or any other language) raises a number of questions. The first of these is at what point a word adopted from a contact language becomes a word of English. Consider a simple case of adoption from French in current British English. The word *baguette* is a relatively recent import into English. The long, crusty loaf (which is what *baguette* means in French) used to be called *French bread*. The term *baguette* was added to the ninth edition of *The Concise Oxford Dictionary* published in 1995, with the meaning of a loaf of bread of a particular shape (the texture is frequently very different from the French original!). My own experience of the word *baguette* in England in 2000 was that it referred to a sandwich made with a piece of French bread, rather than to the loaf itself. I have since seen the same use of the word elsewhere. The question is: is *baguette* an English word? If it means a sandwich, it is no longer recognisable to the French, because its meaning has changed from the original (as well as its pronunciation, although the differences between the French and the English pronunciations are fairly subtle). So perhaps we can say that it is no longer a French word, but an English one. But what if it means the loaf of bread? Is it then a French word being used to denote a French cultural phenomenon, or has it become an English word, and how can one tell? When a word such as *baguette* moves from one language to another, we usually talk about 'borrowing' and 'loan words' (although hijacking might seem a more appropriate metaphor to some). Precisely when a word crosses the boundary from being a foreign word to being a loan word is an unanswerable question, although we get hints from the way the word in question is printed in text: if it is printed in italics, that marks it as being 'other'; unchanged font indicates it is not seen as out of the ordinary. Ultimately, this depends on speakers' attitudes to the word in question.

Perhaps more fundamentally, we have to ask whether an adopted word such as *koala* is a word of a particular variety of English (in this case, a word of Australian English) or whether it is simply a word of English. Koalas are probably discussed more in Australia than they are elsewhere, and in rather different terms (they are more likely to be discussed because of the noise they make than because of how cuddly they look, for example). But English only has the word *koala* for the animal, and a child in Toronto is almost as likely to know the word as a child in Melbourne. This contrasts with a word like *bunyip*. Although bunyips, like koalas, figure in children's literature, the word is much more likely to be known in Australia than in Canada, and phrases such as the *bunyip aristocracy* are likely to be met only in Australia. English only has the word *bunyip* to denote bunyips, too, but the word is likely to be much more restricted in its geographical occurrence. Is it possible to distinguish between words like *koala* which are English, and words like *bunyip* which are Australian English? Again, it seems, not easily, and not by any easily applicable rule. With such words, it is probably less their existence which marks a text as Australian, than their concentration: many mentions of koalas and bunyips (and dingoes, kangaroos, and so on) may suggest an Australian text; an occasional mention may be found in a text from elsewhere.

In this chapter we will go on to consider ways in which varieties of English around the world have acquired new words, some of which (but not all of which) will be recognised in Britain. The use of the words marks a text as belonging to a particular variety only if the words are concentrated in the text.

3.1 Borrowing

3.1.1 Borrowing from aboriginal languages

The most obvious source of new words for new things in the colonial environment was clearly the language of the people who were already on the spot. Although all sorts of myths circulate about English speakers asking 'What is that?' and being told 'I don't know what you mean' and using the word for 'I don't know what you mean' as the name for the new object, there are no authenticated examples of this happening: generally people seem to have made themselves understood well enough. In some places the English speakers did not recognise that the aboriginal peoples spoke a variety of different languages and might justifiably have different words for 'the same thing', but that is a very different problem. Again, it is intuitively fairly obvious that the things newcomers are likely to ask the locals about are 'Where are we?' and then about the unfamiliar phenomena surrounding them, in particular flora, fauna and the arte-

Name	Language	Original version if different	Original meaning
Australia			
Noosa	Gabi-gabi	gnuthuru	ghost
Toorak	Woiwurung	tarook	black crows
Canada			
Manitoba	Ojibwa	manitobah	strait of the spirit
Quebec	Abenaki	quebecq	where the channel narrows
New Zealand			
Otago	Maori	Otakou	place of red ochre
Petone	Maori	pito-one	beach end
South Africa			
Bongani	Xhosa		give thanks
Manzimahle	Zulu		beautiful water
United States			
Chattanooga	Creek	Chatanuga	rock rising to a point
Ticonderoga	Iroquoian	Cheonderoga	between lakes

Figure 3.1 Some borrowed toponyms

facts and practices of the aboriginals themselves. These words will be considered as separate classes, simply because there are so many of them, before other, more general words are looked at.

TOPONYMS

The names of new towns and recently encountered physical features were often chosen by colonisers to remind them of Britain or of the names of their own great people (consider *Boston, Melbourne, Queenstown, Vancouver, Wellington,* and so on). But they also took over large numbers of aboriginal names, sometimes modifying them on the way. Some examples are given in Figure 3.1.

FLORA

A few examples of borrowed names for plants are given in Figure 3.2, along with the language they are taken from. Since the plants themselves are not necessarily known outside their own geographical area, these words may not all be known to you (see question 1 for this chapter), but the general principle is well-established, that local words are used for

Word	Taken from	Original form if different	Original meaning if different
hickory	Algonquian	pocohiquara	drink made from hickory nuts
kauri	Maori		
mulla mulla	Panyjima	mulumulu	
minnerichi	Garuwal	minariji	
mobola	Ndebele	mbola	
squash	Narragansett	asquutasquash	uncooked green
tsamma	Nama	tsamas	
toetoe	Maori		

Figure 3.2 Some borrowed words for flora

Word	Taken from	Original form if different	Original meaning if different
dingo	Dharuk	diŋgu	
kangaroo	Guugu Yimidhirr	gaŋurru	male grey kangaroo
kookaburra	Wiradhuri	gugbarra	
masonja	Shona	masondya	
moose	Abenaki	mos	
raccoon	Algonquian	oroughcun	
skunk	Algonquian	segākw	
tsetse	SeTswana	tsètsè	
tuatara	Maori		
tui	Maori		

Figure 3.3 Some borrowed words for animals

unfamiliar local plants. Not, of course, in every case: sometimes familiar words are used for the new plants, and such cases will be discussed below.

FAUNA

Animals are treated in much the same way as plants, with the same range of possibilities for naming them. Some borrowed words for animals are given in Figure 3.3.

Word	Meaning	Taken from	Original form if different
boomerang		Dharuk	bumarin[y]
bora	initiation ceremony	Kamilaroi	buuru
mere	club	Maori	
muti	African medicine	Zulu	umuthi
mungo	bark canoe	Ngiyambaa	maŋgar
pa	fortified village	Maori	
potlatch	ceremonial giving away of property	Nuu-chah-nulth	patlatsh
powwow	meeting, gathering	Algonquian	powwaw
sangoma	witch doctor	Zulu	isangoma
teepee	conical tent	Sioux	tīpī
tokoloshe	evil spirit	Zulu	utokoloshe

Figure 3.4 Some borrowed words for artefacts and cultural practices

CULTURAL ARTEFACTS AND PRACTICES OF THE ABORIGINAL PEOPLES

Just as unknown as the flora and fauna that are met in the colonial situation are the cultural practices of the local peoples and the physical objects used in them. Sometimes a local custom has an obvious equivalent word, for example a funeral. Occasionally, the local custom seems so foreign that such an equivalent does not seem justified, as with *powwow* (listed in Figure 3.4) or the Maori equivalent *hui*.

OTHER MORE GENERAL WORDS

Although there are obvious reasons for borrowing words for unfamiliar objects and practices, speakers also borrow words for more familiar things. Sometimes this is done because of the perceived foreignness of the object, sometimes it is done because the borrowed word appears particularly useful or suitable (sometimes for reasons which cannot easily be reconstructed). Some examples are given in Figure 3.5.

3.1.2 Borrowing from other types of English

The assumption here has been that speakers of standard British English

Country	Word	Meaning	Taken from	Original form and/or meaning if different
Aus	billabong	blind creek	Wiradhuri	river which runs only after rain
Aus	budgeree	good	Dharuk	bujari
Aus	cooee	call attracting attention	Dharuk	guwi
CDN	hyak	hurry up!, immediately	Chinook Jargon	
CDN	iktas	goods, belongings	Chinook Jargon	
NZ	kia ora	a greeting	Maori	
Aus	koori	Aboriginal man	Awabakel	guri: man
CDN	loshe	good	Chinook Jargon	
SA	mbamba	illicitly brewed liquor	Zulu	bamba: strike with a stick
US	mugwump	a great man	Algonquian	mugquomp: great chief
NZ	puckeroo	broken	Maori	pakaru

Figure 3.5 Some examples of other borrowed words

brought with them to the various colonies the words of standard British English, and enlarged upon that word-stock by borrowing from local languages. But of course that is a simplification. Not only did emigrants from many different regions settle in the new colonies, bringing with them their own non-standard words, there has been continual contact since settlement with the rest of the English-speaking world. For this reason a word that is only dialectal in Britain may nevertheless be standard (or at least widespread) in another national variety, and words which originated outside Britain may have become standard (or widespread) outside their home area (and sometimes in Britain, too). Some examples are given in Figure 3.6. A special case here is the large number of Americanisms, often overtly despised outside North America, but adopted anyway, which have spread not only to Britain but to the rest of the world. Some examples are: *disc-jockey, gangster, gobbledygook, hot-dog, itemize, joy-ride, mail-order, porterhouse steak, sky-scraper, trainee, usherette, vaseline.* The examples have been chosen to show how unremarkable

Country	Word	Original variety	Meaning
Aus	attle	Cornish	refuse from a mine
Aus, NZ	dinkum	Lincolnshire	work, *thence* true, genuine
SA	stroller	Scottish	street kid
Aus, NZ	stroller	US	pushchair
Aus	wild cat (mine)	US	a mine in land not known to be productive
Aus, NZ	youse	Irish	you (pl)

Figure 3.6 Words borrowed from external varieties of English

such innovations seem after several years of constant use. (For further discussion see section 7.1.)

3.1.3 Borrowing from other colonial languages

In Canada, English speakers met French speakers who were already colonising the region; in the United States English speakers met French speakers near the Canadian border and in Louisiana, and Spanish speakers in New Mexico, Texas and California; in South Africa they met Dutch speakers. These contacts also left their traces. Sometimes place-names are those given by other colonisers (*Bloemfontein, Detroit, Los Angeles, Montreal*, and so on). Sometimes English has adopted words for colonial phenomena from another colonial language: *meerkat, melkboom, moegoe* (/mʊxʊ/'country bumpkin', possibly from Bantu) are all taken into South African English from Cape Dutch/Afrikaans. Sometimes words from aboriginal languages passed through one of these other colonial languages before being borrowed into English. Again, words for flora and fauna are numerous in this process. Examples are given in Figure 3.7. Sometimes words were simply taken over from the other colonising language and applied to local phenomena: *armadillo, bonanza, canyon, coyote, palomino, lasso, sarsaparilla, sierra, yucca* are all from Spanish; *ratel, spoor* are from Dutch/Afrikaans; *mush!* (a command to sled dogs) and *gopher* ('ground squirrel') are both from French.

3.1.4 Borrowing from external languages

English is well known as being a language which is very open to borrowing, and this overall tendency remains just as important in colonial

Word	Original Aboriginal language	Original meaning if different
Via French		
bayou	Choctaw	stream
caribou	Mi'kmaq	snow-shoveller
Eskimo	Algonquian	eaters of raw flesh
pichou	Cree	
toboggan	Mi'kmaq	
Via Cape Dutch		
quagga	Khoikhoi	
Via Spanish		
sassafras	origin unknown	

Figure 3.7 Aboriginal terms borrowed into English via other colonial languages

Word	Used in	Origin
bandicoot	SA	Telugu *pandikokku*
depot ('railway station')	US	French
dime	NAm	French
echidna	Aus	Greek, meaning 'viper' (because of the shape of the animal's tongue)
malish ('never mind')	Aus	Egyptian Arabic
padrao ('inscribed pillar')	SA	Portuguese
panga ('cane-cutter's knife')	SA	Swahili
sashay	NAm	French *chassé*

Figure 3.8 External borrowings

Englishes. It is thus not unusual for just one variety of English to borrow from an external language (neither a local aboriginal language, nor a contact colonising language), and for that loan word to be a potential marker of the appropriate variety. Some examples are given in Figure 3.8.

Word/expression	Translated from	Meaning
land of the long white cloud	Maori *Aotearoa*	New Zealand
dreamtime	Aranda *alcheringa*	mythical era when the world was formed
marsh rose	Afrikaans *vleiroos*	
on one's nerves	Afrikaans *op sy senuwees*	tense and likely to get angry
now now	Afrikaans *nou nou*	a moment ago
stay well	Xhosa, Zulu, etc.	farewell
stockfish	Dutch *stokvis*	hake
treesnake	Dutch *boomslang* (also used)	
monkey's wedding	Portuguese	simultaneous rain and shine
mat house	Afrikaans *matjieshuis*	

Figure 3.9 Calques

3.2 Coining

As well as borrowing new vocabulary from other languages, languages all have the ability to generate their own new words and expressions by a number of different means. These are the focus of this section.

3.2.1 Calques: coining on the basis of another language

Calques are also called 'loan translations', and are a kind of half-way house between borrowing and coining. Rather than borrowing a foreign word or expression as is, each part of that expression is translated into English to form a new English expression. South African English seems to have particularly open to this method of gaining new words. Some examples are given in Figure 3.9.

3.2.2 Compounds

By far the most common way of creating new words from the resources of English is by compounding: putting two words together to form a new word. A number of examples from different varieties of English around the world are given in Figure 3.10.

bellbird (Aus, NZ)	monkey orange (SA)	rhinoceros bird (SA)
bloodwood (Aus)	mousebird (SA)	soap opera (US)
boxcar (NAm)	murder house (NZ)	soapbush (SA)
cabbage tree (Aus, NZ, SA)	paper bark (Aus, NAm)	soda fountain (NAm)
catbird (NAm)	parrot fish (SA)	stickfight (SA)
copperhead (Aus, NAm)	rattlesnake (NAm)	wetback (US)
frost boil (CDN)	rest camp (for visitors at	
glare ice (CDN)	a game reserve) (SA)	

Figure 3.10 Examples of compounds formed in varieties of English from around the world

3.2.3 Derivatives

Although compounding is the most common way of forming new words to describe the new situations met by colonists, derivation is also used, perhaps especially in the USA. From Australia we find derivatives such as *arvo, barbie, bathers, watersider*; from Canada words like *hauler*; from New Zealand words such as *gummy, scratchie, sharemilker* and *ropable* (which is also used in Australia); from South Africa comes *outie*; and *accessorize, beautician, burglarize, hospitalize, mortician, realtor, winterize* are all from the USA.

3.2.4 Other word-formation processes

There are a number of processes besides compounding and derivation which can be used to form new words, and these processes can give rise to words which are identified with one particular variety of English. Clipping gives us *gas, gym, movie, narc, stereo* (all originally from the USA); blending gives us *motel* and *stagflation* (both originally from the USA); back-formation gives us *commute, electrocute* (both originally from the USA). Clipping with suffixation gives us New Zealand English *pluty* 'posh'. And imitation gives us Australian *mopoke* 'species of owl'. Every country has its own sets of initialisms and acronyms referring to local institutions.

3.2.5 Changes of meaning

As well as the creation of new forms, vocabulary expansion can take place by giving new meanings to old forms. Again, these new meanings may be specific to one geographical area. For example, *ash* and *mahogany* are both used in Australia to apply to many eucalypts; *badger* was used in Australia to refer to marsupials, especially the wombat, and *mole* was sometimes used in the nineteenth century to refer to the platypus; *robin* is used to refer to a number of different species of bird in North America, Australia and New Zealand; a *barber* may be a sheep-shearer in Australia; in South Africa a *block* is a number of farms in a single unit owned by one person or company and an *excuse-me* is a derogatory term for an educated, middle-class person. *Bikkies* is used in Australia and New Zealand to mean 'money' especially in the phrase *big bikkies*, 'a lot of money'.

3.2.6 Changes of style

Sometimes it is not so much that the meaning of an existing word changes, but just that its style-level changes. In New Zealand, the word *untold* is not at all poetical, but an everyday word meaning 'many' (frequently with the stress on the first syllable), and, as in South Africa, the word *varsity* is an ordinary student word for a university, not just an upper-class word as in Britain.

The USA has seen the coining of a number of words which are intended as jokey words, words which have sometimes spread beyond the USA to other varieties of English. Examples are: *absquatulate, bodacious, cahoots, catawumpus, hornswoggle, rambunctious, splendiferous.*

3.2.7 Descriptions

If all else fails, it is always possible to give a description of a new phenomenon, and let the description stand as its name. Some examples (from various countries) are given in Figure 3.11.

3.3 The results

3.3.1 Heteronymy

The term 'heteronymy' is from Görlach (1990b) and refers to the situation where the same item is referred to by a number of different words. A simple example is provided by what is called a *lorry* in Britain, which is called a *truck* in Canada, the USA, Australia and New Zealand. Equally what in Britain is called a *pavement* is called a *sidewalk* in Canada and the USA and a *footpath* in Australia and New Zealand. Each of these terms can be referred to as a heteronym. Although usage is changing

bald eagle	US
brown gannet	Aus
brown snake	Aus
lemon-scented gum	Aus
pallid cuckoo	Aus
spotted kiwi	NZ

Figure 3.11 Descriptions used as names

USA	England	Australia/New Zealand
garters (to hold up a woman's stockings)	suspenders	
jumper	pinafore dress	
knickers	plus-fours	
panties	knickers	pants
pants	trousers	
shorts	(under)pants	
suspenders	braces	
sweater	jersey, jumper	
turtle-neck shirt	polo-neck shirt	skivvy
undershirt	vest	singlet
vest	waistcoat	

Figure 3.12 Heteronymy in names for items of clothing

rapidly, articles of clothing used to provide a rich field for heteronymy, as illustrated in Figure 3.12. The situation is simplified in Figure 3.12 by ignoring variation in each of the areas considered and giving only the main word used (sometimes in rather conservative usage).

In Figure 3.12 it will be seen that words such as *suspenders*, *pants* and *vest* can have different meanings depending on where (or by whom) they are used. Görlach (1990b) calls such words 'tautonyms' – words with the same form but different meanings.

3.3.2 Polysemy

One result of extending the meanings of already existing words is an increase in polysemy; in other words, there are more words with several meanings. Polysemy also arises through other types of coining, where the same form is coined in different places to refer to different objects. The case of the word *robin* has already been mentioned. The British robin is *Erithacus rubecula*; the American robin is *Turdus migratorius* (that is, it is related to the thrush); in Australia there are several birds called a *robin*, including the dusky robin (*Melanodryas vittata*), the scarlet robin (*Petroica multicolor*) and the yellow robin (*Eöpsaltria australis*); in New Zealand there are two robins, the New Zealand robin (*Petroica australis*), and the Chatham Island or black robin (*Petroica traversi*).

There are bellbirds in Australia and in New Zealand; but while they are of the same family, the Australian bellbird is *Manorina melanophrys* and the New Zealand one is *Anthornis melanura*. There are also South American bellbirds.

The word *cabbage tree* in South Africa refers to members of the species *Cussonia*, in Australia to members of genera *Corypha*, and in New Zealand to *Cordyline australis*.

Exercises

1. Look up the words you do not know from Figures 3.2, 3.3 and 3.7. Which countries are they used in? What do they mean?

2. Look for some more heteronyms, this time in the names for items of food. Where is each of the labels used?

3. What variety of English is the following text written in? How can you tell?

> The man seemed to sigh, stuck the boomerang into the strip of animal skin that was his belt and, in fact, the whole of his wardrobe, and stood up. Then he picked up a leathery sack, slung it over one shoulder, took the spears and, without a backward glance, ambled off around a rock.
> …
> 'You want some grub?' The voice was almost a whisper.
> R[.] looked around. A little way off was the hole from which last night's supper had been dug. Apart from that, there was nothing all the way to the infinite horizon but scrubby bushes and hot red rocks.
> 'I think I dug most of them up,' he said weakly.
> 'Nah, mate. I got to tell you the secret of finding tucker in the bush. There's always a beaut feed if you know where to look, mate.'

4. It was stated that the data given in Figure 3.12 was dated. For any one variety of English, see if you can discover how far the data presented was

and still is true. You can either try checking in dictionaries, or you can ask people of your own, your parents' and your grandparents' generations what they say or used to say.

5. Benor (1999) gives, among others, the following words borrowed from Hebrew, Yiddish and Aramaic, used by Ashkenazic modern orthodox Jews in North America.

maxloxet	argument	dɑfkʌ	to spite someone with intent
talɪs	prayer shawl	kipʌ	skull cap
koʃər	ritually acceptable (of food)	sfʌrɪm	religious books
ʃiər	lesson	ləvɑjʌ	funeral
mɪnhʌg	tradition	ʌsər	forbidden

To what extent can you see the same forces operating in these borrowings as in borrowings in the colonial setting, and to what extent are these different? Why?

Recommendations for reading

There are major dictionaries of Australian (Ramson 1988), Canadian (Avis 1967), New Zealand (Orsman 1997) and South African (Silva 1996) Englishes. Ironically, there is no dictionary of British usage (though there are specialist dictionaries of Scottish and Irish usage), since most British works include American usages, and vice versa. However there are dictionaries which provide translations for the uninitiated, and point out instances of tautonyms (Moss 1984; Zvidadze 1983); there are also useful lists in Benson et al. (1986).

4 Grammar

It is only recently, with the advent of large computer corpora of reasonably representative materials from a number of varieties of English around the world, that it has become possible to discuss difference in grammar at all meaningfully. While many people are familiar with a very small number of differences, it was not always clear, before statistical treatments of such matters could be given, how much variation there was, and how many of the distinctions were absolute. The result of a few decades of corpus-based studies has largely been disappointing: there tend not to be striking absolute grammatical differences between national varieties. Rather it seems to be the case that where speakers of one variety prefer structure *a*, and speakers of another prefer structure *b*, both *a* and *b* are available to speakers of both varieties. As an example, consider the following.

In a study looking at the use of synthetic (*friendlier, friendliest*) and analytic (*more friendly, most friendly*) comparison of adjectives ending in *-ly* in the American newspaper *The New York Times* and the British newspaper *The Independent*, Lindquist (2000) shows, for example, that the British paper is a little more likely than the American one to use the synthetic form in attributive position (that is, premodifying a noun, as in *the friendliest person*) as opposed to in predicative position (*he was friendliest*). The figures are given in Table 4.1.

What results like those in Table 4.1 show is that British and American Englishes (at least as illustrated by these two newspapers) are very similar in their use of synthetic and analytic comparison, and that where there are differences, they are of a kind which can be discovered only by considering a large body of data, not just by looking at an individual example. Such results are typical.

4.1 Morphology

English has a handful of irregular plural forms of nouns: *oxen, brethren, children, men, women, feet, geese, teeth, lice, mice*. These do not vary from

Table 4.1 Attributive and predicative usage of synthetic and analytic comparison in two newspapers (from Lindquist 2000)

| | | The New York Times | | The Independent | |
		% attrib.	% predic.	% attrib.	% predic.
Comparative	synthetic	51	49	55	45
	analytic	44	56	37	63
Superlative	synthetic	88	12	96	4
	analytic	84	16	89	11

(The table is to be read such that 51 per cent of synthetic comparatives in *The New York Times* are attributive, and 49 per cent of them are predicative, etc.)

variety to variety, except that in New Zealand English *women* is becoming homophonous with *woman*, leading to confusion of spelling. English also borrows a lot of nouns from Latin, Italian, French and other languages, and these sometimes retain their foreign plurals: *tableaux, tempi, alumni, cherubim* and so on. Such plurals are often variable within a variety, but there is no reported case of national varieties being distinctive in terms of which plural they choose (despite the fact that this might seem a natural potential site for such variation). Similarly, English sometimes shows variation between an unmarked plural form for huntable/edible animals and a marked one (*fish* is probably the most variable noun, but consider also *deer, sheep* and *salmon*, which are less variable, and *antelope, duck*, which show a lot of variation – mainly semantically or pragmatically based). Again, such variability is not known to distinguish national varieties of English. There is also a set of nouns in English whose base form ends in a voiceless fricative and which make their plural by irregularly voicing that fricative and then adding the plural ending: *house, wolf* and *wreath* are clear examples. These are known to be variable both within varieties and between varieties. *Roof* is notorious for having a prescribed regular plural, *roofs*, while many speakers voice the plural and thus write *rooves*. The Disney version of *Snow White* featured seven *dwarves*, which caused some confusion in Britain where *dwarfs* was the normal plural, though Tolkien has *dwarves*. British English allows *wharfs*, while the plural in New Zealand is exclusively *wharves*. It is notable that the irregular forms mentioned here come from outside England: the normal trend in morphology is for the forms outside Britain to become regularised.

The variation in nominal morphology is trivial in comparison with the variation in verbal morphology. English has a large set of irregular verbs. On the whole, this set has been getting smaller since the common Germanic period: modern English has considerably fewer than Old

English had, for example. But there was always a fair amount of variation in these forms. In standard forms of the language, this variation decreased in the eighteenth century as part of the movement to 'fix' the language. Forms from the range in actual use at that period were artificially selected, sometimes arbitrarily, and became the 'correct' form in the standard language. Many of the alternatives continued to be used in non-standard varieties, which is why things like *We seen it*, *She done it* are still so common today. Sometimes the forms selected seem illogical: why should it be (in the English of England) *We have got it* but *We have forgotten it*? In Figure 4.1 a list of verbs which show some variation related to regional variety is given. Despite the markings that are given in Table 4.1, it is often the case that either form can be found in both the USA and in the UK; the marking shows preferences rather than absolutes. Unmarked examples are found everywhere. Australia and New Zealand typically show both types, sometimes with a preference for the British form (such as *spoilt*), sometimes with a preference for the American one (for example *dreamed*). Only standard forms are listed here: things like *She swum across the bay* are heard, but are rarely found in print.

Derivational morphology is largely the same throughout the English-speaking world. Diminutives in *-ie* are more frequent in Australasia than in most other places, and this tendency may have been inherited from Scottish English. *Rellies* for 'relatives, relations', for example, is an Australasian form. Some diminutives in *-ie* are found in other areas as well, though. Similarly, although the use of the suffix *-ee* as in *muggee*, *murderee* is more common in the USA than in other areas, the suffix is known and productive everywhere.

In principle we might expect to find derivational affixes used and accepted in only one country. This seems not to happen. Either an affix which is rare elsewhere is used more in one particular country (as with the *-ie* mentioned above, or with the Australian *-o* in words such as *garbo* 'dustman, garbage collector' or *journo* 'journalist'; this suffix is known in Britain in words like *ammo* and *beano*), or an affix is used mostly in one country, but the words produced by that affix are freely used elsewhere (as with the words on the pattern of *beatnik* such as *peacenik*, *refusenik* which were coined mainly in the USA).

4.2 Syntax

If there is very little syntax which can be used unambiguously to point to the particular origin of a text, there is nonetheless a lot of syntax which is variable, and where in principle a good statistical analysis of a large enough text could provide enough information to say where it originated.

beat	beat	beaten	
beat	bet	beaten	esp. Scotland, NZ
bet	bet	bet	
bet	betted	betted	esp. UK
burn	burned	burned	US
burn	burnt	burnt	UK
dive	dived	dived	
dive	dove	dived	only US and CDN
dream	dreamed	dreamed	esp. US
dream	dreamt	dreamt	esp. UK
dwell	dwelled	dwelled	US
dwell	dwelt	dwelt	UK
get	got	got	
get	got	gotten	US (not in all senses)
kneel	kneeled	kneeled	esp. US
kneel	knelt	knelt	
lean	leaned	leaned	esp. US
lean	leant	leant	esp. UK
leap	leaped	leaped	esp. US
leap	leapt	leapt	
learn	learnt	learnt	UK
learn	learned	learned	US
prove	proved	proved	
prove	proved	proven	esp. US, Scotland, NZ
shine	shined	shined	esp. US or = 'polish'
shine	shone	shone	UK /ʃɒn/, US /ʃoːn/, CDN usu. /ʃɑːn/
smell	smelled	smelled	US
smell	smelt	smelt	UK
sneak	sneaked	sneaked	
sneak	snuck	sneaked	esp. US and CDN
spell	spelled	spelled	US
spell	spelt	spelt	UK
spill	spilled	spilled	US
spill	spilt	spilt	UK
spit	spat	spat	
spit	spit	spit	US only
spoil	spoilt	spoilt	UK
spoil	spoiled	spoiled	US
swell	swelled	swollen	UK, US
swell	swelled	swelled	UK, US
thrive	thrived	thrived	esp. US
thrive	throve	thrived	

Figure 4.1 Some variable verbs

4.2.1 Sentence structure

There is variation in the relative order of direct and indirect objects when these are both pronouns: some speakers can say *give it me* while others can only have *give me it*. Quirk *et al.* (1985: 1396) say that the former is only British English, but the comparison they make is exclusively with American English. Trudgill and Hannah (1994: 67) say that *give it me* is only northern, even in England (though the map in Cheshire *et al.* 1989: 203 shows that it is not quite as simple as northern versus southern). Everyone can have, and may prefer, *give it to me*.

So-called collective nouns, such as *government, committee, team* may take either singular or plural concord, either on a verb where such words are the subject, or in agreement with a later pronoun.

(1) The company *is* able to provide 80 customer carparks at Ngauranga. (*The Evening Post* [Wellington, New Zealand] 2 April 1984, p. 8 col. 6) (singular concord)
(2) The number two computer company worldwide *require* a sales representative. (*The Evening Post* [Wellington, New Zealand] 14 April 1984, p. 17 col. 3) (plural concord)

Through most of the twentieth century, it was claimed that British and American Englishes were distinguished in this way, with British using plural concord. In the course of the twentieth century, singular concord became more common in some types of British text, though not all collective nouns have changed at the same speed. *Government*, for example, is far more likely to be used with singular concord than *police*. On top of this, variation in singular or plural concord may have social implications in some places. Singular concord is now the norm with at least some of these collective nouns in formal newspaper usage the USA, England, Australia and New Zealand. In Australian English, this use of singular concord is spreading to sports teams, so that even a sports team with a plural name may be used with singular concord, as in (3) (Newbrook 2001: 120).

(3) The Kangaroos [= North Melbourne] must improve *its* percentage.

The use of the unmarked verb stem, called the mandative subjunctive (see section 1.3, Quirk *et al.* 1985: 155–7), in sentences like (4) is also variable between varieties. US English uses the subjunctive more than British English, which tends to prefer to use the modal *should* instead (as in (4′)), and may use an indicative verb (with concord marked, as in (4″)). New Zealand and Australian English show an intermediate level of subjunctive use in such cases. (For a good summary, see Hundt 1998: 89-97.)

(4) I order that all experiments in Mordon *cease* forthwith and that the buildings *be* bulldozed to rubble. (Alistair MacLean, *The Satan Bug*, London and Glasgow: Fontana, 1962: 90)

(4′) I order that all experiments in Mordon *should cease* forthwith and that the buildings *should be* bulldozed to rubble.

(4″) I order that all experiments in Mordon *cease* forthwith and that the buildings *are* bulldozed to rubble.

There is variation in commands beginning with the word *go* between such things as *Go jump in a lake!* and *Go and jump in a lake!* As is pointed out by Taylor (1989: 239), the version with no *and* is borrowed into Australian English only where it has abusive function. *Go and see who is at the door* has no alternative form in Australian English.

In South African English, a sentence-initial *no* is often found where it would not be used in most other varieties. Its value is to contradict the assumptions made in the preceding part of the dialogue (Branford 1994: 489; Trudgill and Hannah 1994: 32). Examples are given in (5).

(5) 'Can you deliver it?'
'No, sure, we'll send it this afternoon.'

'How are you?'
'No, I'm fine, thanks.'

4.2.2 Auxiliary verbs

One of the points of variation most often cited with reference to auxiliary verbs is the use of the modal auxiliary *shall* (and, to a lesser extent, *should*). The use of *shall* is usually seen as being particularly connected with the standard English of England; Australian (Trudgill and Hannah 1994: 19; Newbrook 2001: 129), New Zealand (Trudgill and Hannah 1994: 26; Hundt 1998: 58–61) Scottish and US Englishes (Trudgill and Hannah 1994: 59, 97) gain particular mention in the literature as those varieties which avoid *shall*, and use *will* in place of it. The degree to which the word *shall* is avoided (and the contexts in which it is avoided) is variable. Hundt (1998: 59) provides figures to suggest that New Zealand English is the least likely to use *shall*, but does not include Scottish English in her comparisons.

The verbs *dare* and *need* are unusual in that they can act either as main verbs (in which case they are followed by an infinitive with *to* – compare *want* in (6)) or as modal auxiliaries (in which case they are followed by a bare stem verb – compare *must* in (6)).

(6) We want to come. (main verb)
   We must come. (auxiliary)
(7) He didn't dare to look. (main verb)
   He didn't dare look. (auxiliary)
(8) Does she need to be here early? (main verb)
   Need she be here early? (auxiliary)
(9) All you need to do is tell it like it is. (main verb)
   All you need do is tell it like it is. (attested. Hundt 1998: 64)
   (auxiliary)

According to Trudgill and Hannah (1994: 61), US English does not have
the auxiliary construction with these verbs, although other evidence (for
example Hundt 1998: 62–3) suggests that this is an overstatement of the
case, and that it would be better to say that the auxiliary construction is
rare in US English. Collins (1989: 143–4) finds that *need* and *dare* are not
used in precisely parallel ways in Australian English: *need* is used as a
main verb, but while *dare* is more often found with the *do*-verb, it tends
to be used without the *to*, leading to a mixed type. Similar results for *dare*
are found by Bauer (1989a) for New Zealand English, though respondents accepted both the auxiliary and the main verb construction for
need. Hundt's (1998: 63) figures for both New Zealand English and the
English of England suggest that whether *need* is in affirmative, negative
or interrogative sentences has a major effect on the construction actually
used.

Similar problems beset *used to*. Although speakers may not be sure
whether to write *use to* or *used to* to represent /juːstə/, this marginal
modal provides no problems in the affirmative (10). In the negative (11)
and interrogative (12), however, there is variability.

(10) I used to like olives.
(11) I didn't use(d) to like olives. (main verb)
   I used not to like olives. (auxiliary)
   I usen't to like olives. (auxiliary)
(12) Did you use(d) to like olives? (main verb)
   Used you to like olives? (auxiliary)
   Used you like olives? (auxiliary)

Usage in Australia is divided (Collins 1989: 144; Newbrook 2001:
116–17), though the use of the relevant form of *do* appears to be favoured
in New Zealand English (Bauer 1989a: 11–14). In England, there are
stylistic differences between the various options such that *I usen't to like
olives* is more formal than the other options, and to a certain extent this
distinction is passed on to the colonies, including the USA. The forms

with *do* are sometimes ascribed to American usage (Newbrook 2001: 117), but have clearly become the norm beyond the USA, and even in Britain in informal usage.

The semi-modal *ought (to)* presents a very interesting case of variability. First, it seems to be less used now than it used to be, being replaced by *should*. Second, it is used variably with and without the following *to*. And third, if it is repeated in a tag question there is variability in what form occurs.

(13) I ought to know the answer to that question.
      Yes, you ought.
      Yes, you ought to.
(14) You didn't ought to do that.
      You oughtn't to do that.
      You oughtn't do that.
(15) Ought we to send for the police?
      Ought we send for the police?
(16) I ought to know the answer to that, oughtn't I?
      I ought to know the answer to that, shouldn't I?
      I ought to know the answer to that, didn't I?

The various patterns are not all well described. According to Quirk *et al.* (1985: 139-40), *ought* without *to* is preferred by both British and American informants in interrogatives and negatives, and *didn't ought* is not readily used. The same is true in Australian English (Collins 1989: 142). There it is also the case that although *ought* is recognised, *should* is more often used. In New Zealand English (Bauer 1989a: 10) *should* is preferred, and is used in tags even where *ought* is maintained. The tag question with *did* (illustrated in (16)) is given as British by Trudgill and Hannah (1994: 19), but is not mentioned by Quirk *et al.* (1985: 812).

In South African English, the progressive may be marked by the expression *be busy*, as in *We're busy waiting for him now* (Branford 1994: 490). This is a rare calque of an Afrikaans construction which has been picked up in English, and its origin explains why it is not used elsewhere.

4.2.3 Complementation

In English we can say both *I believed that he was guilty* and *I suspected that he was guilty*. But while we can equally say *I believed him guilty*, we cannot say **I suspected him guilty*. The particular patterns a verb can take, whether it is intransitive, transitive or ditransitive, what kind of preposition follows it, what finite or non-finite clause pattern it requires, is a matter of complementation. In some cases, complementation depends on the meaning: the difference between *she's baking* (intransitive), *she's baking a cake* (transitive) and *she's baking me a cake* (ditransitive) is clearly determined by meaning. But the *suspect/believe* distinction illustrated above is not related to meaning, but is an idiosyncratic feature of the individual verb, and as such it is open to variation (see Miller 2002: 49–52).

In practice, it is only the complementation patterns of a few verbs which are usually considered in this context, although there may be more variation here than we are aware of: on the whole we do not have enough information about the alternatives (such as that following *believe*) to know whether there is any regional variation in the way in which they are used. Each verb will be treated individually below, looking at them in alphabetical order.

Appeal. We are not concerned here with the use illustrated in *Her sense of humour appealed to me*, but in legal senses of *appeal*, often extended to the sporting arena. In British English, this is an intransitive verb, followed by the preposition *against*; in Australian and New Zealand it is also a transitive verb: *They appealed the decision.* The transitive use replaces the use with *against* in US English.

Explain. Explain may be ditransitive in South Africa: *Explain me this* (Lanham 1982: 341).

Farewell. It is not clear whether *farewell* is really a verb in many varieties of English, but in Australian and New Zealand Englishes it clearly is, and it is transitive: *We farewelled Chris, who's moving to Greenland, last night.*

Fill. In US English you tend to *fill out* the forms which, in British English, you would be more likely to *fill in*. Australian and New Zealand Englishes allow both.

Progress. Progress can be an intransitive verb everywhere: *The matter is progressing slowly.* However, a transitive use is beginning to be heard, possibly everywhere: *We are hoping to progress this matter.*

Protest. Protest is rather like *appeal*. While US English tends to prefer the construction *We protested the decision*, British English is more likely to use *We protested against the decision* (with the possibility of using *at* or *about* instead of *against*). Australian and New Zealand Englishes allow both.

Reply. Reply may be transitive in South African English: *He didn't reply me* (Lanham 1982: 341).

Screen. Hundt (1998) draws attention to the fact that New Zealanders (and to a lesser extent Australians) are perfectly familiar with the construction *The new James Bond film will screen next week*, while this is not familiar to British or American respondents (although a few examples were found in one US source). Transitive use of *screen* is general, as in *We will screen the new James Bond film in our largest theatre.*

Visit. Visit with someone is attested in Britain in the nineteenth century (for example, George Eliot uses it in *Middlemarch*), but now appears to be virtually only used in US English (see the *Oxford English Dictionary*).

Want. Many varieties influenced by Scottish English permit the construction illustrated in *The dog wants out*, and also permit *These clothes want* (or *need*) *washed*. This appears to be dialectal in the USA (see for example LINGUIST List 2.555, 25 September 1991), as it also is in New Zealand.

You may be able to find further examples, though in many cases you need to be careful in pinning down the place where the variation occurs: for example everyone uses *meet with* in *Our cat met with an accident*, but *meet with* can be in variation with transitive *meet* for people meeting other people (but perhaps not on all occasions). I don't think you would *meet with* someone quite by accident on the way to the shops; *meet with* tends to be equivalent to *have a meeting with*, and thus to be more specific than transitive *meet*.

4.2.4 Have

There is variation between *have* and *have got*, so that both (17) and (18) are possible. When such sentences are negated or questioned, this gives rise to the range of possibilities shown in (19) and (20).

(17) He has a cold/a new car.
(18) He has got a cold/a new car.
(19) I haven't a cold/a new car.
      I don't have a cold/a new car.
      I haven't got a cold/a new car.
(20) Have you a cold/a new car?
      Do you have a cold/a new car?
      Have you got a cold/a new car?

These may or may not be completely synonymous. There could be a distinction between *I have a new car* (implying 'I wouldn't lower myself to drive around in a used vehicle') and *I've got a new car* (meaning 'I have just acquired a vehicle which I used not to own'). Trudgill and Hannah (1994: 63) point out another possible difference in meaning between *Have you (got) any fresh cod?* (meaning 'Is there any fresh cod in the shop?') and *Do you have fresh cod?* (meaning 'Do you generally stock fresh cod?'). However, it seems that for most speakers these distinctions are not regularly maintained.

This variation also works with *have to* meaning 'must'. So we find structures equivalent to those in (20) like those in (21).

(21) Have you to leave immediately?
      Do you have to leave immediately?
      Have you got to leave immediately?

There are also differences of style, such that versions with *got* are more likely to occur in less formal language, with the result that they are often commoner in speech than in writing.

Despite all this variation, there is also variation here based on variety of English. For example, US English seems to use *do*-support in questions and negatives far more than British English does, and the same is true for Australian and New Zealand Englishes (Bauer 1989b; Collins 1989; Hundt 1998; Quinn 2000). The use of variants with *got* seems to be more common in New Zealand spoken English than in British spoken English (Bauer 1989b).

At the same time, there is evidence of ongoing change in this part of the grammar. All varieties seem to be adopting *have got* forms in the meaning illustrated in (21) (Hundt 1998: 55). Some of the variation between different varieties may be accounted for in terms of different speeds of adoption of this form rather than because the varieties have different established norms.

4.2.5 Noun phrases

There has been a change in the course of the twentieth century in journalistic texts from the construction illustrated in (22) to the construction illustrated in (23) (Barber 1964: 142; Strevens 1972: 50; Trudgill and Hannah 1994: 75):

(22) Margaret Thatcher, the British Prime Minister, arrived in Washington today.
(23) British Prime Minister Margaret Thatcher arrived in Washington today.

The difference may be motivated by the (marginal) gain in space. Whatever the reason, the change appears to be better established in US English than in British English.

There are some nouns, like *church*, which do not require an article in certain constructions where an article would otherwise be expected: *go to church* is good English, but **go to town hall* is not. Which nouns behave like *church* is a matter which can change from variety to variety. *Be in hospital* is good British English, but not good American English, and the same is true of *be at* or *go to university*. On the other hand *be in* or *go to class* is probably more usual in US texts than in British ones (Strevens 1972: 52,

Trudgill and Hannah 1994: 74). Similarly with musical instruments, following the verbs *learn* and *play* there is variation between using and not using *the*: *I play (the) piano.*

The indefinite pronoun *one* is rare in any but the most formal writing, and in less formal styles is replaced by an indefinite *you*. Its use to mean 'I' seems to be virtually restricted to British royalty. But where it genuinely means 'someone unspecified' it can be followed in US English, but not in British English, by *he* or *she*.

(24) It simply does not follow that if *one* believes that abortion is murder then *he* would advocate killing individual abortionists. (From Koukl 1994; my italics LB)

The sentence in (24) could only appear in an American text; in a British text the italicised *he* would have to be *one*.

4.2.6 Prepositions

Choice of preposition is often variable, as we have already seen with regard to complementation patterns. Even where there is no preceding verb, though, there can be variation in the use of prepositions, and, indeed, in whether a preposition is used or not.

Traditional British *at the weekend* has yielded in the last fifty years or so to the American *on the weekend*, although other prepositions such as *during, over* and (in New Zealand English) *in* are also possible in the same construction.

Other similar differences are found in the expressions *Monday to/through Friday, Ten to/of/till nine, Quarter past/after ten, to be in/on the team*, and so on.

In many temporal expressions, US English can omit a preposition that is necessary in other varieties: *I'll see you (on) Friday, (On) Saturdays, we like to go fishing, (At/on) weekends, we play golf, The term starts (on) March 1st, He works (by) day(s) and studies (at) night(s)*. In each case the shorter version started out being a US variant, but has been adopted to some extent in other parts of the world (Strevens 1972: 51; Trudgill and Hannah 1994: 80).

4.2.7 Adverbs

Where prepositions are omitted in phrases like *She works nights, nights* becomes an adverb. Such constructions have already been considered.

In some varieties of English, *already* and *yet* can co-occur with a verb in the simple past tense, as in (25); in other varieties a perfect is required (26).

(25) I ate already.
      Did you eat yet?
(26) I have already eaten.
      Have you eaten yet?
      (Trudgill and Hannah 1994: 77)

In both Canadian and Australian Englishes, possibly also in South African English, *as well* can occur sentence-initially, as in *As well, there are three other cases of this* (Trudgill and Hannah 1994: 78; Newbrook 2001: 128). Why this feature should arise in precisely those three varieties and not in others (assuming that it is not found elsewhere) is something of a mystery.

4.3 Discussion

The list of features that has been given in this chapter is clearly not a complete list. Trudgill and Hannah (1994) list far more variable grammatical features, for example. Nevertheless, we can take it that the kinds of variability that have been listed here are reasonably representative of the kinds of variation that are found within inner circle Englishes.

What is striking about most of these features is how superficial they are. For example, patterns of complementation and prepositional choices are virtually matters of vocabulary: whether you say *in the week-end*, *on the weekend* or *at the weekend* is something that depends on the noun *weekend*, and has no obvious influence on other phrases; similarly, whether you *protest a decision* or *protest against the decision* depends on the verb *protest*, and need not spread beyond that individual word. The use of the definite article is not under threat in its core usages, it is only in a few expressions in very specific semantic fields that there is variation in its use. The use of auxiliaries illustrates stages in the development of a system where two forms have already become synonymous, and there is an attempt to sort out the synonymy: if *ought to* and *should* mean the same thing, perhaps it should be possible to use *should* in tag questions to *ought*, and we may not need *ought* at all; if *shall* just means *will*, they may not both be needed. In none of these cases is the system getting a major upheaval; rather adjustments are being made round the fringes.

When we come to consider the degree to which English is breaking up into a number of daughter languages in section 8.5, it will be useful to bear this in mind: there is no lack of variation in grammatical features, but the places where there is variation are not the major areas of the grammar.

It can also be argued that many of the changes are simplifications. This is most obvious in the verbal morphology illustrated in Figure 4.1, where the colonial version tends to be the regular version. However, a change from *Have you any money?* to *Do you have any money?* is also a simplification, in that it makes *have* just like other transitive verbs: we would say *Did you spend any money?*, not *Spent you any money?*

Exercises

1. As a class exercise, take two newspapers published in different countries and mark every occurrence of each of the variables discussed in this chapter. Does the variation go in the expected direction? What other comments do you have on the exercise?

2. What prepositions (if any) do you use in the following sentences?
a) I always win ___ rummy.
b) We are studying ___ dinosaurs at school.
c) We tried to prevent the hecklers ___ becoming a nuisance by splitting them up.
d) You have to stop her ___ turning up at all hours of the day or night.
e) She threw it ___ the window.
f) We live ___ Burberry Street.
g) I haven't seen him ___ ages.
h) He fell ___ his horse.
i) They incline ___ laziness.
j) They have found jobs ___ a nightclub.
k) We were sitting ___ the veranda, enjoying the view.
l) We need to deal ___ the matter promptly.
m) There are a couple ___ people I want to see.

3. Choose any one syntactic feature discussed in this chapter and decide whether the colonial variant is or is not a simplification in respect of the Home variant.

4. Good data on sentences like (17) to (20) can be very difficult to obtain for several reasons: (a) the constructions tend to be rare; (b) it is not always clear precisely what the speaker/writer intended the meaning to be; (c) people use constructions differently in speech and in writing; and so on. How would you attempt to carry out a fair survey of the differences in usage in this area from two varieties of English?

Recommendations for reading

Trudgill and Hannah (1994) is worth looking at, though it deals with varieties individually and it may be difficult to see the generalities. A harder book to read, but a worthwhile one, is Hundt (1998). Although this is ostensibly about New Zealand English, Hundt considers Australian and US Englishes as well, making comparison with British varieties. She also puts forward the hypothesis that what is different between the varieties she considers is speed of change rather than the nature of the changes themselves.

5 Spelling

Given the stress that is laid on spelling by prescriptivists, and the existence of so many dictionaries which provide standard spellings for English words, it is perhaps surprising that there should be any variation in spelling within standard varieties. But there is. Some of this variation is variation between varieties. More often, though, there is variation within a variety. The pattern of variation, however, is not the same in every variety. The result is that in principle, given enough data, we would be able to distinguish varieties on their spelling habits. In practice, at least on the basis of a very small sample, this is less possible than people might think.

The major distinction is usually drawn between British and American spelling conventions. Let us begin by making the simplifying assumption that this is all we have to worry about. Given just these two varieties, we have the following possible cases:

- Both varieties spell a word the same way: *cat.*
- The two varieties spell a word in different ways: *honor/honour.*
- American English allows either of two spellings for a word, British English allows only one: *ax/axe.*
- British English allows either of two spellings for a word, American English allows only one: *generalise/generalize.*
- Both varieties allow variation in spelling for a word (though possibly not in the same proportions): *judgment/judgement.*

We can also analyse the variation in another dimension: does the variation apply to just one word – in the terms used to discuss pronunciation (see section 6.7.4), is it a matter of lexical distribution (for example *grey/gray*) – or is there a generalisable pattern (*honor/honour*)?

While dealing with these five types of comparison might be simple enough with just two varieties, once we try to deal with half-a-dozen things become more difficult. Perhaps fortunately, southern hemisphere varieties tend to follow British patterns in spelling, and only Canadian

English stands out as requiring clearly different treatment from British and US varieties. Accordingly, southern hemisphere varieties will be discussed here in terms of deviation from the British standards. Comments on US, British, Australian and New Zealand Englishes are based on corpus studies; South African English is not mentioned specifically here; it tends to follow British norms; comments on Canadian English are based on Pratt (1993) and Fee and McAlpine (1997).

5.1 Lexical distributional differences

By 'lexical distributional differences' we refer to differences which affect a single lexical item (or word) and where the difference is not part of a general pattern. A list of relevant words and where they are used is provided in Figure 5.1. In a case like *tire/tyre*, where *tyre* is used only of wheel-parts, but *tire* can also mean 'to fatigue', it is to be understood that the meaning with the restricted spelling (here 'wheel-part') is the one intended.

5.2 Variation in the system

5.2.1 *<ise>/<ize>*

There is a common misapprehension that -*ize* (and -*ization*) is American, while -*ise* (and -*isation*) is British. Oxford University Press continues to prefer -*ize* for its house style, and many British publishers allow either. American and Canadian publishers restrict themselves to -*ize*. Australian and New Zealand publishers tend to use -*ise* rather more consistently than their British counterparts, with <z> spellings usually being a sign of learned or scientific writing in those varieties. Prescriptive statements on the matter (for example Weiner and Hawkins 1984) say that the <z> spelling may be used only in the -*ize* suffix, derived from Greek, and that words like *supervise* (from Latin), *surprise* (from French) and *merchandise* (from French) cannot take the <z> spellings. However, of these, only *supervise* is not listed with a <z> in American dictionaries, and even that can be found spelt with a <z> on the internet (apparently especially from educationalists!) – though rather inconsistently, see Markham (1995).

5.2.2 *<our>/<or>*

One of the ways in which Webster fixed American spelling was in making it standard to have no unnecessary <u> in words like *colour* and *honour*. (For further discussion of Webster, see section 8.2.) This remains a good

Spelling 1	Spelling 2	US	GB	CDN	Comment
artifact	artefact	1	1, 2	1	
ax	axe	1, 2	2	2	
check	cheque	1	2	2	
curb	kerb	1	2	1	
disk	disc	1, 2	1, 2	1, 2	Computer disks are universally spelt with a <k>. The meaning of 'record' or 'CD' is usually spelt with <c> in Britain, but <k> in the US and Canada.
draft	draught	1	2	1	*draft a letter* is so spelt everywhere; other kinds of *draught* vary.
gray	grey	1, 2	2	2	
jail	gaol	1	1, 2	1	
mustache	moustache	1, 2	2	2	
net	nett	1	1	1	*nett* is a conservative norm, still used in Australasia.
pajamas	pyjamas	1	2	1, 2	
plow	plough	1	2	1, 2	
skeptic	sceptic	1	2	1, 2	
story	storey	1	2	2	
sulfur	sulphur	1, 2	2	2	
tire	tyre	1	2	1	
wagon	waggon	1	1, 2	1	Australasian usage seems to prefer variant 1.

Figure 5.1 Lexical spelling mismatches in British, US and Canadian English

means of telling the two varieties apart: outside proper names from the other system, British writers very rarely omit the <u>, and US writers rarely include it. Canadians here usually choose the US variant, New Zealanders choose the British variant. In Australia, however, usage is divided and both variants are found. Butler (2001: 160) reports that

'Two thirds of the nation's newspapers use the *color* spelling and only one third use *colour*, but Australians almost universally write *colour*.' The Australian Labor Party is so spelt.

5.2.3 <re>/<er>

The use of <er> and the end of words like *centre* and *theatre* is another of Webster's pieces of standardisation, and again a valuable one for distinguishing British and US writings. In this case, however, Canadians regularly use the British variant, and Australians and New Zealanders use the <re> spellings in relevant words consistently.

5.2.4 Consonant doubling

If you add a suffix to a verb like *travel* in British English, you usually double the <l>, to give *travelled, travelling, traveller*. Americans double the <l> only if the vowel immediately preceding the <l> carries stress: *compelling* but *traveling*. The exception is *woollen/woolen*, where the single <l> spelling in US English is (despite what has just been said) regular: although it is at the end of a stressed syllable, that syllable contains a vowel sound written with two vowel letters, and should thus work like *beaten*. While this distinction is most noticeable with the letter <l> it also applies to other letters, though not necessarily so consistently. Americans can write either *kidnaping* or *kidnapping*, either *worshiping* or *worshipping*, and everybody writes *handicapped* but *paralleled*. With the words *biassed* and *focussed*, everyone now prefers the single <s> variant, which follows the US rules, although the <ss> variants are still used in Britain.

Ironically, in a few words with final stress, usage in Britain tends to prefer a single <l> (which still gets doubled when an affix is added) while in the USA the double <ll> is preferred: *distil(l), enrol(l), enthral(l), extol(l), fulfil(l), instil(l)*. None of these words is particularly common. Australian and New Zealand usage seems to be split on these words.

Canadians tend to prefer the British spellings for all of these words.

5.2.5 <ce>/<se>

There are two distinct sets of words where the difference between an <s> and a <c> becomes significant.

The first concerns words which are viewed as parallel to *advice* and *advise*. Here the noun has a <c> where the verb has an <s>. *Practice* and *practise* are treated in British English as though they are differentiated in the same way (despite the fact that there is no parallel difference in pronunciation). In the USA both are spelt with a <c>. The distinction between *licence* and *license* is treated in the same away in British English, while the two are again spelt the same way in the USA, but this time both with an <s>. Actual usage is not entirely consistent in any country considered, with deviations from the expectations outlined above going in both directions.

The second set of words contains only nouns such as *offence/offense, defence/defense, pretence/pretense*. Here only the <c> variant is used in Britain, while the <s> variant is preferred in the USA. Note that this explains the US spelling of the noun *license* mentioned above. This differentiation is much better maintained than the *practice/practise* one just described.

Canadians prefer the British options in all of this except for the verb *practice*, but there is variation, perhaps especially in the word *offence/offense*.

5.2.6 <ae> and <oe>

When <ae> and <oe> are pronounced /iː/ (sometimes /e/), the usual US practice is to spell them with <e>. Thus we find variation in words such as *encyclop(a)edia, f(a)eces, h(a)emoglobin, medi(a)eval* and in *diarrh(o)ea, f(o)etid, f(o)etus, (o)estrogen*. Canadian journalistic writing usually prefers the US spelling here, though academic writing may not. It is hard to give a general statement for these words. Many are changing in Britain and the southern hemisphere to the American spellings, but the change is not equally rapid for all: *encyclopedia* is often seen spelt thus even in British-influenced territories, while *oestrogen* is more likely to maintain the classical spelling.

5.2.7 Base-final <e>

Consider a pair of words such as *like* and *liking*. The final <e> on like is to 'make the vowel <i> say its name' (as this is often phrased in primary teaching). This final <e> is not required when another vowel follows the <k>, as in *liking*. The <i> in the suffix fulfils the same purpose. Now consider *courage* and *courageous*. The vowel following the <g> is sufficient to make the stressed <a> in *courageous* 'say its name', but we still need the <e> to make the letter <g> into [dʒ] rather than [g]. Similarly, a <c> before <a>, <o> or <u> will signal [k] rather than [s].

If we put these together, then *likable* should require no <e>, while *placeable* from the verb *place* should require one (*placable* is a different word, related to *placate*, and pronounced with a [k] and a short [a]).

Despite these general rules, there is a frequent spelling of words like *judg(e)ment* with no medial <e> after the <g>. The <dg> is obviously felt to be sufficient to mark the [dʒ] sound. The variation affects very few words (*acknowledgement, judgement, fledgeling*), and both spellings are found in both British and American English. However, the variant with no <e> is rather more common in North America, while the variant with an <e> is rather more common elsewhere.

While, in accordance with the rules, *movable* and *unmistakable* are clearly dominant spellings in print, spellings such as *moveable* and *unmistakeable* are also increasingly found. They occur only where the root of the suffixed form is a single syllable (*move, take*), and not where the root has more syllables – *debatable* does not retain the <e> of *debate*. These new spellings are found especially in Australasia and in Britain. The same is true of similar spellings with the affix *-y: jok(e)y, shak(e)y, ston(e)y*, and so on. Although <c> and <g> do not need an <e> before <y>, the <e> is still often retained in words like *poncey* and *rangey*.

5.2.8 <y> or <i>

There are a number of words where a <y> is preferred in British spelling while an <i> is permitted in US spelling. The words include *cypher/cipher, gypsy/gipsy, pygmy/pigmy, sylvan/silvan, syphon/siphon* and *syrup/sirup*. Most of these words are so rare that actual usage is difficult to gauge, but it seems to vary from item to item, and to be slightly inconsistent on both sides of the Atlantic.

5.2.9 <x> or <ct>

There are a few words like *connexion/connection, inflexion/inflection* where there is variation between <x> and <ct>. Both spellings are found in all varieties of English, but with a preference for the <ct> variant in all, and <x> being particularly rare in the US and Australia. Given the existence of words like *collection* with only one spelling, the <x> variant seems likely to continue to get rarer.

5.3 Conclusion

The spellings discussed above do not exhaust the variable spellings found in English. No mention has been made of respellings such as *donut, lite, nite, tho, thru,* for example, of the difference between *hankie* and *hanky*, or the distinction between *whisky* and *whiskey*, which may carry semantic weight as well as indicating where a text is produced.

As with grammar, there are very few sure-fire ways of recognising a particular variety of English from the spelling. As with grammar, if we had sufficient data to produce a statistical profile, we could start to make informed guesses. As with vocabulary, it is often easier to use spelling to say where a text was not produced than to pinpoint its origin. National origins do affect the spelling in a text, but the correlation is frequently not quite as straightforward as may appear to the uninformed eye.

Exercises

1. Although it is often hard to tell precisely which country a given spelling might be found in, some combinations provide very strong evidence. The spelling 'Tire Centre', for instance, is likely to be seen in only one country. Which country? Why?

2. Consider the following brief text, and say what can be deduced about its origin on the basis of the spelling.

> Such a picture is not all that far from reality for some of [our] biggest subsidised performing companies in opera, dance, music, circus and theatre. So last year the ... Government set up a Major Performing Arts Inquiry ... to look into the financial position of these, the nation's premier performing companies, and to propose options for improving their prospects. The inquiry's Discussion Paper, released last week, is the most significant document bearing on ... cultural policy since the Labor Government's Creative Nation statement in 1994.

3. How straightforward a task would it be to program a computer to take a document spelt in the British manner and turn it into one spelt in the American manner or vice versa?

4. The rather unnatural sentence below has been concocted to illustrate a number of points of orthographic variability. Identify the points in question. If you change them one at a time, do you end up with a sentence which could have been produced by a consistent writer, or do some spellings imply others?

> I like to fantasise that someone does me the sizeable honour of providing me with a travelling scholarship to visit the Centre for Gypsy Studies.

5. In natural texts, the features of spelling discussed in this chapter

rarely occur with sufficient concentration to let you determine anything from a brief text such as that given in question 2. Choose a random text written in a variety of English which is not the one you feel most familiar with, and see how much help you can get from the spelling in determining the national origin of the text. Is it different for different types of text? In your texts, would vocabulary or spelling be better guides to telling you where the text is from?

Recommendations for reading

The best general book on English spelling is Carney (1994). Although Carney does not discuss spelling from our point of view, he does discuss places where there is variation, and often discusses the British/American split.

6 Pronunciation

Although it may be true that people believe that all Americans say *the hood of a car* where all Britons say *the bonnet of a car*, such features are scattered enough in real text not to be primary indicators of national variety. That honour belongs to pronunciation. On the basis of pronunciation – and a remarkably small sample of pronunciation at that – we are willing to place almost any speaker in the English-speaking world. We may not get it right: in particular United States and Canadian accents can be difficult to distinguish, as can Australian and New Zealand ones for outsiders (and sometimes for the locals, see Weatherall *et al.* 1998), and many Americans find it hard to tell the Southern Hemisphere varieties apart from British ones.

In this chapter we will consider problems involved in describing and comparing varieties of English in terms of their pronunciation; we will look at the kinds of influences that have led to the current pronunciations of varieties around the world, and discuss the kinds of pronunciation phenomena that you can encounter when describing a variety of English or when comparing two of them.

6.1 Describing varieties of English

Typically, accents of English are described in terms of deviations from one of the two best-described accents, RP and General American. RP, or Received Pronunciation, is the non-regional and upper-class accent of England, described in handbooks such as Jones (1918) and Gimson (1962); General American (GA) is an idealised version of the accent which is most widespread in the United States, specifically excluding features which mark the speaker as coming from New England, New York, or the linguistic South. GA is described in handbooks such as Larsen and Walker (1930), and in Kenyon and Knott (1953) is referred to, rather misleadingly, as 'northern'. These two varieties are chosen as reference varieties because they are so well described, and because they are the prestige varieties in their own areas of influence. This manner of describing accents has the advantage that most scholars of English accents are reasonably familiar with one or both of these accents, and can relate easily to descriptions given in terms of them.

There are at least two problems with such an approach. The first is that it is theoretically dubious. Each variety has its own system, and in principle the systems of the individual varieties are no more comparable than the systems of Swahili and Basque. In some ways, however, this argument might be seen as naive. Whatever the fine theoretical principles are, all inner circle varieties of English are derived from a small number of closely related originals, share large amounts of vocabulary, and tend to have related pronunciations in the same lexical items. For that reason, Wells (1982) introduced the notion of lexical sets. Lexical sets are groups of words which share a particular phoneme in most varieties of English. Each set is named by a word which illustrates the phoneme in question. For instance, the lexical set BATH includes words such as *bath, path, pass, laugh, castle, shaft*, and so on. These words are all pronounced with /ɑː/ in RP and with /æ/ in GA, but the assumption is that in any given variety they will behave in the same way. There is another lexical set START which contains words such as *start, cart, heart, marsupial, cartilage* and *remark*. The BATH lexical set and the START lexical set are pronounced with the same vowel phoneme in RP, but not in GA. Lexical sets are thus not to be equated with phonemes, and so the theoretical problems mentioned above do not occur when we describe accents in terms of them. At the same time, they allow for comparisons across varieties in a useful way. Wells sets up lexical sets only for vowels, though in principle lexical sets for consonants could also be established: for example, we might want to set up WHELP and WENT lexical sets for those varieties (like Scottish English) which distinguish between *witch* and *which*, or a LOCH lexical set for those varieties which have a velar fricative in words like *loch*. It is also the case that the lexical sets which Wells establishes are not sufficient for all varieties. For example, in many varieties of New Zealand English, *goad, god* and *gold* all have phonemically distinct vowels pronounced [gʌud], [gɒd] and [gɒud] respectively. We need to set up a lexical set (which we could perhaps call COLT) to allow this distinction to be discussed. It is not clear how many lexical sets would be required altogether. Wells' selection is provided for reference in Figure 6.1. For the sake of brevity, and following usual practice, a phrase such as 'the vowel occurring in the BATH lexical set' will frequently be abbreviated in what follows to 'the BATH vowel'.

The second reason why comparing all accents with either RP or GA is problematical is that it is historically incorrect. RP is an upper-class

Note that the words denoting the sets have been chosen (a) so as not to be easily confused with each other, (b) to be monosyllables, usually ending with a voiceless obstruent.

KIT	BATH	THOUGHT	NEAR	HAPPY
DRESS	CLOTH	GOAT	SQUARE	LETTER
TRAP	NURSE	GOOSE	START	COMMA
LOT	FLEECE	PRICE	NORTH	
STRUT	FACE	CHOICE	FORCE	
FOOT	PALM	MOUTH	CURE	

Figure 6.1 Wells' lexical sets

accent in origin, and the people who provided the basis for the most widespread accents of Australia, New Zealand or South Africa were not upper-class people. Whatever they spoke, it was not the direct fore-runner of RP. Moreover, in origin at least, RP was a London accent, the accent of the court and the professions. If we oversimplify, we can imagine RP and Cockney having had a similar origin, but having developed along slightly different lines. For many purposes we are really more interested in the parent-accent of both Cockney and RP than we are in either of these modern varieties. Unfortunately, we have little direct evidence about what that variety might have been like.

The use of Wells' lexical sets is the best way of avoiding both these traps. Even though the lexical sets tend to reflect historical classes, and tend to reflect particular sound-changes which have taken place in the histories of individual varieties, they nevertheless provide a relatively neutral vocabulary which avoids presuppositions. These lexical sets will be used in the discussion from now on.

6.2 Input varieties

The fundamental assumption about varieties of English in the colonies (see section 1.2) must be that their accents have developed in some way from the accents of the speakers who first established the appropriate colony. This is no more than an assumption: the accent may have been more strongly influenced by the accent of a larger, neighbouring colony, the colony may have self-consciously tried to adopt some accent foreign to many of its original members, the accent will almost certainly have been modified by the speech of later immigrants. Nevertheless, if we do not make this assumption, we have very little on which to base any discussion whatsoever. Now, in most cases we know a lot less than we would like to know about the linguistic background of those early colonisers. We may know that they came from several parts of the south of England or Scotland, for example. But we also know that accents in England and Scotland may change considerably within a five-mile (eight-kilometre) radius, and we rarely know (a) precisely how many speakers from any particular area there were or (b) precisely where the people came from. In some ways, then, we are forced to do some linguistic detective work: 'if this is the current make-up of the local accent,' we have to ask, 'what can the input varieties have been?' Answering this question demands that we understand what happens in the process of dialect mixture (see the discussion in section 1.4).

Dialect mixture is the process that occurs when speakers with two or more different accents come together and speak to each other. The mixture can occur on two levels. On the micro-level, I change my accent to talk to you (this is usually called 'accommodation'). On the macro-level, the children who grow up in a society with no established accent of its own speak with a new accent which reflects some of the features of all the inputs. It is this macro-level mixture which is the most important when we are talking about accent-formation in new colonies, but the macro-level mixture is based on precisely the kinds of modifications that we all make when we accommodate to other speakers.

Thanks in particular to work done by Trudgill (1986), we know of some general principles which speakers seem to follow when accommodating to each other, and according to which new dialects are formed out of old ones. Some of these principles may be ones which you yourself have experienced in dealing with people who talk a different way from the way you do. You may or may not 'hear yourself' talk differently to different addressees, or hear members of your family adjust their speech (for example on the telephone) depending on the accent of their interlocutors.

- Where a lot of accents come together, it will be expected that the majority form will win out; 'majority' here may be interpreted in terms of the widest social usage.
- A form is more likely to win out if it is supported by the spelling system.
- Forms intermediate between competing original forms may arise.
- Phonological contrasts are more likely to be lost than gained.
- An increase in regularity is to be expected.
- Phonetically difficult sounds are likely to be eliminated.
- Variants which originate in different dialects may become specialised as markers of social class in the new accent.

6.3 Influences from contact languages

In the instances being discussed in this book, the English speakers formed a large enough community to maintain English as their primary language. Since the original colonists would be adult, they would not adapt their English much to the local languages. While their children would have the possibility of learning other surrounding languages, they would also have before them a model of English which paid little attention to the phonetics and phonology of the contact languages. Even today, when it is seen as politically correct to pronounce the aboriginal languages in the aboriginal way, the pronunciations that are heard are strongly influenced by English, even among the group of speakers who make a genuine attempt to conform to non-English models.

In New Zealand, early spellings indicate that words borrowed from the Maori language, the language of the indigenous people of New Zealand, were pronounced in a very anglified way. For instance, Orsman (1997) notes several spellings for Maori *ponga* [pɔŋa] 'type of tree fern': *ponga, pongo, punga, ponja, bunga, bunger, bungie, bungy*. Some of these spellings may reflect varying pronunciations in the different dialects of Maori. The use of <b> for Maori /p/, however, is an indication that the unaspirated /p/ of Maori was perceived in English terms rather than in terms of the Maori phonological system. Similarly, the frequent /ŋg/ pronunciations in medial position arise from treating this word as a simple word like English *finger*, rather than from listening carefully to the Maori pronunciation. Such uninformed pronunciations are still common in colloquial New Zealand English, but in the media Maori words (and, perhaps especially, Maori placenames) have been 'dis-assimilated' or 'de-Anglicised' (Gordon and Deverson 1998: 121) to a more Maori-like pronunciation. Toponyms such as *Raetihi*, *Te Kauwhata* or *Wanganui* provide good test cases. They are pronounced /rɑːtəˈhiː, tiːkəˈwɒtə, wɒŋɡəˈnjuːiː/ in unself-conscious colloquial usage, but /ˈraɪtɪhiː, tɪˈkaʊfʌtə, wɒŋəˈnuːiː/ in more Maorified media-speak. Even this latter pronunciation is, of course, not Maori: it is merely a closer approximation to the Maori pronunciation of these names.

Similarly, in Canada it is becoming more frequent to see words borrowed from the First Peoples (as the Canadian Indians are now called) being spelt according to the conventions of the languages concerned – which often leads to a new pronunciation in English. Thus the people who used to be called *Micmac Indians*, are now called *Mi'kmaq* (singular *Mi'kmaw*); the Chippewyans would now refer to themselves as members of the Dene nation (since *Chippewyan* was an English version of the Cree name for their people); similarly, the people who used to be called the *Ojibwa(y)*, now prefer to be called *Ashinabe* ('people'), which is their own name for their people (Fee and McAlpine 1997). With a pair such as *Thompson* and *Nlaka'pamux*, these differences are as much lexical as they are phonological. But the difference between *Ottawa* and *Odawa* is purely phonological.

In rare cases, contact can lead to the introduction of a new phoneme into English. South African English has a phoneme /x/ in a number of loan words. While most of these are Afrikaans words, some are Khoikhoi words, possibly mediated by Afrikaans: *gabba* /xaba/ 'friend' and *gatvol* /xatfɒl/ 'fed up, disgusted'. The addition of /x/ to English speech is perhaps not all that foreign, since it is already used in Scottish and Irish varieties of English, and this may have made its adoption easier.

6.4 Influences from other colonies

During the colonial period, contact between colonies was often arduous, and restricted to a small section of the populace. The linguistic results of such contacts would be expected to be minimal, and in general terms that is true. There are, however, some notable exceptions, which it is worth mentioning.

There were originally several independent settlements in North America (in Nova Scotia, in New England and in Jamestown, Virginia), with each settlement having its own distinctive make-up in terms of the origins of the migrants. The linguistic differences between these various groups can still be heard today. However, in the later stages of settlement, the Northern and Southern settlements in the present United States met. While the two can still be distinguished on dialect maps (see, for example, the data on *bristle* in the questions for Chapter 2), and even in terms of building styles (Kniffen and Glassie 1966, cited in Carver 1987: 10), nonetheless there must have been considerable mutual influence between the two groups.

The second notable exception is the influence between United States English and Canadian English. Many of the original Canadian settlers came from what is now the United States, and it is only natural that they should have spoken in the same way as their southern neighbours. While they tried to maintain their separateness in their language as well as their politics (a separateness which has led to many discussions of Canadian spelling over the years, for example – see Chapter 5), most Canadians still live very close to the United States and have regular contact with the United States. It is therefore not all that surprising that most outsiders can't tell the difference between Canadian and US Englishes.

The third notable exception is provided by Australia and New

Zealand. Although these two countries are a lot further apart than most people from the Northern Hemisphere realise, at approximately 1,200 miles (2,200km), nearly all trade and immigration to New Zealand came via Australia in the early days. In the 1860s the quickest route between Wellington and Auckland (the two main cities in New Zealand, approximately 500km apart as the crow flies) was by a 4,000km round trip via Sydney, and there were many Australians in New Zealand, particularly in the early days of settlement and through the gold rush of the 1860s. There is considerable evidence that much vocabulary is shared between Australia and New Zealand (Bauer 1994a), and again the accents, while not identical, are similar enough for outsiders not to be able to distinguish them.

6.5 Influences from later immigrants

British immigration into Australia, New Zealand and South Africa has been a continuing phenomenon. Immigrants to these countries, moreover, still thought of themselves as being British until well through the twentieth century. While the American Declaration of Independence in 1776 meant that from that date onwards Americans no longer looked toward Britain as a spiritual home, in Australia and New Zealand the word *Home* was still used with reference to Britain into the 1960s, though the usage died out a bit earlier in South Africa. This meant that people in the southern hemisphere colonies still cared about the situation in Britain and still wanted to sound as though they belonged to Britain until surprisingly recently – indeed, as far as the sounding like is concerned, it is not clear that all members of all the communities have given up on that aim even yet, and the broadcast media in Australasia still use British RP as a standard to which they aspire (Bell 1977), if less than previously. Under such circumstances, we can understand why RP is still given high social status and why no equivalent local varieties have emerged.

6.6 Influences from world English

During the Second World War (1939–45), when American troops were stationed in Europe and in the Pacific, they discovered that they had great difficulty in communicating with the local English-speaking populace. England and America really were two countries separated by the same language (as George Bernard Shaw once put it). Some of the problems were lexical, many were phonological. With the post-war developments first in radio and then in TV and the movies, it is hard to imagine that being a problem to the same extent today: American English is heard so regularly throughout the English-speaking world, that it has become comprehensible, even prestigious, despite remaining 'other'. People who travelled enough to be familiar with the other idiom have rarely had great difficulty, and reading has never been a major problem. But the actual speech of Americans was once as much a problem as the pronunciation of unfamiliar varieties remains today. English people or southern hemisphere speakers visiting the southern American states can find the people less comprehensible than the Scots and the Irish, while Americans can have trouble understanding people from the north of England or from Australasia on first acquaintance.

What is less clear, however, is the extent to which pronunciations from other varieties have any levelling effect on English world-wide; it may be that alternatives simply remain alternatives ('you like tomayto and I like to-mah-to', as Ira Gershwin wrote in another context). There are certainly cases where one or another variant becomes dominant for a while. In New Zealand, during the cervical cancer enquiry of 1987, *cervical* was regularly pronounced with the PRICE vowel in the second syllable, which was stressed, while in the second enquiry of 1999–2000, the word was usually pronounced with the KIT vowel in the second syllable and the stress on the first syllable. When the American TV programme *Dynasty* was screened in New Zealand in the 1980s, the word was regularly pronounced with the PRICE vowel in the first syllable, though more recently it has reverted to having the (traditional British) KIT vowel there. More permanently, *schedule* seems to be losing its pronunciation with an initial /ʃ/ in favour of the American pronunciation with initial /sk/, *lieutenant* seems, away from the armed forces, to be /luːtɛnənt/ rather than /lɛftɛnənt/, and *nephew* seems virtually to have lost its medial /v/ in favour of /f/ in most varieties of English. The very fact that we can talk of a small number of such cases seems to imply that there is no general movement to do away with variation. This is considered again in Chapter 7.

6.7 Differences between varieties

Wells (1982) provides a classification for pronunciation differences between varieties which holds just as well for colonial varieties as it does for local accents. Varieties, he says, may have different pronunciations because of:

- phonetic realisation
- phonotactic distribution
- phonemic systems
- lexical distribution.

Each of these will be considered in turn.

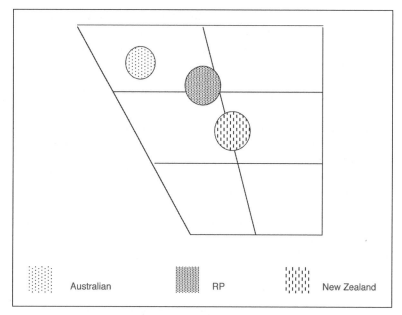

Figure 6.2 The KIT vowel in three varieties of English

6.7.1 Phonetic realisation

Phonetic realisation refers to the details of pronunciation of a sound which may, nevertheless, appear in the same lexical set in two varieties. Two specific examples will be considered here: the KIT vowel, and the medial consonant in ETHER.

The KIT vowel is a well-known shibboleth for distinguishing Australians from New Zealanders. Australians accuse New Zealanders of saying *fush and chups* for *fish and chips*, while New Zealanders think that Australians say *feesh and cheeps*. Neither is correct, because in both cases they make the mistake of attributing the words *fish* and *chips* to the wrong lexical sets. For both Australians and New Zealanders (as for Britons and North Americans) *fish* and *chips* both belong to the KIT lexical set, not to the STRUT set or the FLEECE set. Accordingly, *sick*, *suck* and *seek* are all pronounced differently for both parties. What is different, though, is the phonetic detail of the way in which the KIT vowel is pronounced; and the lay perceptions show the general direction of the phonetic difference. This is illustrated in Figure 6.2, which shows the pronunciation of the KIT vowel in Australian and New Zealand English and in RP.

The fricative in the middle of ETHER is usually pronounced in RP with the tongue behind the top incisors, while in California, the normal pronunciation is with the tongue tip extruding slightly between the teeth (Ladefoged and Maddieson 1996: 143). The normal New Zealand pronunciation is like the Californian one; information is not easily available on other varieties. This difference is not audible to most speakers, and very few speakers are aware of this potential variability. Nevertheless, there are phonetic differences here in the way that particular sounds are produced.

The category of phonetic realisation also includes those cases where one variety has major allophones which another does not have, or a different range of allophones. For example, Canadian English is well known for distinguishing the vowels in *lout* and *loud* ([ləʊt] and [laʊd] respectively) in a way which does not happen in standard varieties elsewhere. RP has a more palatalised version of /l/ before a vowel, while most other standard international varieties have a rather darker version of /l/ in this position (even if they make a distinction similar to the one in RP between the two /l/s in words like *lull* or *little*).

6.7.2 Phonotactic distribution

Phonotactic distribution refers to the ways in which sounds can cooccur in words. The major phonotactic division of English accents is made between rhotic (or 'r-ful') and non-rhotic (or 'r-less') accents (see section 1.4). The difference hinges on the pronunciation or non-pronunciation of an /r/ sound when there is an orthographic <r> but no following vowel. Rhotic accents use an /r/ sound in *far down the lane* as well as in *far away in the distance*; non-rhotic accents have no consonant /r/ in the former (although the vowel sound in *far* reflects the <ar> spelling). GA, Canadian, Scottish and Irish varieties of English are rhotic, as is the English in a small area in the south of New Zealand; RP, Australian, New Zealand and South African Englishes are non-rhotic, as is the English in parts of the Atlantic States in the United States (stereotypically, the accent of Boston Brahmins, who are reputed to say 'pahk the cah in Hahvahd Yahd' for *park the car in Harvard Yard*). The words *heart* and *hot* differ only in the vowel quality in RP, but only in the presence versus absence of an /r/ in GA (and in both features in Scottish English). This difference of rhoticity has some unexpected by-products in that, for example,

- only non-rhotic accents have an /r/ in the middle of *drawing* (/drɔːrɪŋ/);
- speakers of non-rhotic accents trying to imitate an American accent are likely to put an /r/ on the end of a word like *data*, which has no /r/ for Americans;

- only in varieties that maintain the /r/ are words such as *horse* and *hoarse* kept distinct, as /hɔːrs/ and /hoːrs/ respectively in GA; in non-rhotic varieties these words have become homophones.

Another matter of phonotactic distribution is whether the HAPPY vowel is associated with the KIT vowel or the FLEECE vowel. Increasingly, English speakers all round the world think that the word *needy* has the same vowel sound occurring twice in it, though there are some older RP speakers, and some speakers of GA who have two different vowels in the two syllables of such words.

There are some phonetic environments where phonemes contrast in one variety of English but not in another, with the result that homophones in one variety are distinguished in another (and this is predictable on the basis of the phonetic context). The phenomenon is known as neutralisation (see McMahon 2002: 58–60).

For example, in some varieties of North American English, the SQUARE, DRESS and TRAP vowels are not distinguished where there is a following /r/. So *Mary, merry* and *marry* are homophonous in these varieties, although they are all phonemically distinct in RP. In New Zealand English *Mary* and *merry* may be homophonous, but *marry* is distinct. In varieties where this happens, the SQUARE, DRESS and TRAP vowels are still kept distinct elsewhere.

The TRAP and DRESS vowels are not distinct for many speakers of New Zealand English if there is a following /l/, so that *Alan* and *Ellen* are homophones for these speakers. The same is also true for some Australians, but these words are phonemically distinct for most other speakers. Even for speakers who do not distinguish between *Alan* and *Ellen*, the words *sad* and *said* are phonemically distinct.

6.7.3 Phonemic systems

For our purposes, the phonemic system for a particular variety is based on the minimum number of symbols needed to transcribe that variety. Another way of looking at this is to ask which of the lexical sets in Figure 6.1 have 'the same vowel' in them. We do not have a corresponding list of lexical sets for consonants, but the parallel process involves determining for each variety how many distinct lexical sets are required. Consider the partial systems illustrated in Figure 6.3, and the distribution of phonemes among the lexical sets. It can be seen in Figure 6.3 that RP requires four phonemes for these particular lexical sets, GA just three, and Scottish English also three, but a different three. Some varieties of North American English have the same vowel in the THOUGHT lexical set

Lexical set	RP	GA	Scottish
GOAT	oʊ	oː	o
FORCE	ɔː	oː	o
THOUGHT	ɔː	ɔː	ɒ
PALM	ɑː	ɑː	a
LOT	ɒ	ɑː	ɒ

Figure 6.3 Three phonemic systems for dealing with some lexical sets

free and *three*	no distinction made by some non-standard varieties in Britain, Australia and New Zealand
where and *wear*	distinguished in some conservative accents of New Zealand and the US, regularly distinguished in Scotland and Ireland except by some young speakers
lock and *loch*	distinguished in Scotland, Ireland and South Africa
tide and *tied*	distinct in Scottish English, due to the effect of the Scottish Vowel Length Rule (see section 2.3.3)
beer and *bear*	often not distinguished in New Zealand English
moor and *more*	often not distinguished in the English of England
kit and *bit*	often do not rhyme in South African English
scented and *centred*	not distinguished in Australian, New Zealand and South African Englishes; distinguished by vowel quality in RP; distinguished by the absence versus the presence of /r/ in standard North American varieties

Figure 6.4 Further points of phonological difference

as in the LOT lexical set, and require only two phonemes for this part of the system.

Phonemic systems have implications for rhymes: for Tom Lehrer (Lehrer 1965) the following lines have a perfect rhyme

We'll try to stay serene and calm
When Alabama gets the bomb.

because the PALM lexical set and the LOT lexical set are phonemically identical in his variety of English. Since they are different in my variety of English (which is like RP in this regard), the couplet quoted above is not a good rhyme for me.

While there are many aspects of phonemic structure that are shared by the varieties of English discussed in this book, there are, on top of those illustrated in Figure 6.3, places where there are differences (see Figure 6.4 for some examples).

Word	Lexical set to which the stressed vowel belongs in different varieties					
	RP	GA	CDN	Aus	NZ	SA
auction	THOUGHT ~ LOT	THOUGHT ~ PALM	THOUGHT = LOT = PALM	LOT	LOT	THOUGHT
floral	FORCE	FORCE	FORCE ~ LOT	LOT ~ FORCE	LOT	FORCE ~ LOT
geyser	FLEECE	PRICE	PRICE	FLEECE ~ PRICE	PRICE	PRICE ~ FACE ~ FLEECE
lever	FLEECE	DRESS ~ FLEECE	FLEECE ~ DRESS	FLEECE	FLEECE	FLEECE
maroon	GOOSE	GOOSE	GOOSE	GOAT ~ GOOSE	GOOSE ~ GOAT	GOOSE
proven	GOOSE ~ GOAT	GOOSE ~ GOAT	GOOSE	GOOSE	GOOSE ~ GOAT	GOOSE
vitamin	KIT	PRICE	PRICE	PRICE ~ KIT	PRICE	KIT ~ PRICE
year	NEAR ~ NURSE	NEAR	NEAR	NEAR	NEAR	NEAR ~ NURSE

Figure 6.5 Lexical set assignments of a few words in different varieties

Word	Lexical set to which the marked unstressed vowel belongs in different varieties					
	RP	GA	CDN	Aus	NZ	SA
Birming**ha**m	COMMA	TRAP	TRAP	COMMA	COMMA	COMMA
cerem**o**ny	COMMA	GOAT	GOAT	COMMA	GOAT ~ COMMA	COMMA
fert**i**le	PRICE	COMMA ~ Ø	PRICE ~ COMMA ~ Ø	PRICE	PRICE	PRICE
monast**e**ry	COMMA ~ Ø	DRESS	DRESS	COMMA ~ Ø	Ø	COMMA ~ Ø
secret**a**ry	COMMA ~ Ø	DRESS	DRESS	COMMA ~ Ø	DRESS ~ Ø	COMMA ~ Ø
territ**o**ry	COMMA ~ Ø	FORCE	FORCE	COMMA ~ Ø	FORCE ~ Ø	COMMA ~ Ø

Figure 6.6 Lexical set assignments of a few words in different varieties: unstressed vowels

Word	RP	GA	CDN	Aus	NZ	SA
Pronunciation of the marked consonant(s) in different varieties						
a**ss**ume	sj	s	s ~ sj	sj ~ ʃ	ʃ ~ sj ~ s	sj
fi**gu**re	g	gj	gj ~ g	g	g	g
herb	h	Ø	h ~ Ø	h	h	h
ne**ph**ew	f ~ v	f	f	f ~ v	f	f ~ v
quarter	kw	kw	kw ~ k	kw	k ~ kw	kw
schedule	ʃ	sk	sk ~ ʃ	ʃ ~ sk	sk ~ ʃ	ʃ
thither	ð	ð ~ θ	ð	ð	θ ~ ð	ð
wi**th**	ð	ð ~ θ	θ ~ ð	ð ~ θ	θ	ð

Figure 6.7 Consonantal difference between a few words in different
varieties

6.7.4 Lexical distribution

Lexical distribution is the kind of pronunciation difference which is
most easily noticed and commented on. This is the case where one
variety puts a particular word in a different lexical set from another.
Thus in RP the word *tomato* has its second (stressed) vowel in the PALM
lexical set, while in GA it is in the FACE lexical set. The important point
here is that there is no general pattern to observe, it is simply a matter of
individual words behaving in particular ways (often for good historical
reasons). A few examples are given in Figure 6.5, where '~' indicates
'is in variation with', that is both are heard, and '=' indicates that the
various lexical sets are phonemically identical.

Just as often, it is vowels in unstressed syllables that vary. A few
examples are given in Figure 6.6. And some examples of consonant
differences are given in Figure 6.7. In these figures 'Ø' indicates zero,
meaning the relevant segment is not pronounced.

Exercises

1. What kind of difference in pronunciation is the most important
in allowing you as someone who hears different varieties of English to
locate a speaker as coming from a particular country?

2. This chapter has focused on differences in segments (consonants
and vowels). What other kinds of differences in pronunciation may be
relevant?

3. What differentiates the way you speak from either British RP or General American? Give five features.

4. Many lay people tend to treat all pronunciation differences as though they were differences in lexical distribution. For example, they may say of Australians and New Zealanders that 'They say *pen* instead of *pan*'. Yet this is really a difference of phonetic realisation: Australian and (especially) New Zealand TRAP is close enough to sound very similar to RP DRESS everywhere it occurs. Which of the following are genuinely matters of lexical distribution, and which are something else? If the example does not show lexical distribution, what kind of difference is it?

a) Americans and many Australians make *dance* rhyme with *manse*.
b) Some old-fashioned New Zealanders still say /basɪk/ for *basic* in some contexts.
c) In Canada, *Don* sounds like *Dawn*.
d) Australians say *to die* when they mean *today*.
e) English people say *to-MAH-to* and not *to-MAY-to*.
f) For many speakers of English, *real* sounds just like *reel*.

Recommendations for reading

Trudgill and Hannah (1994) discuss the pronunciation of individual varieties of English, comparing each with RP. For non-American varieties, the individual chapters in Burchfield (1994) are useful. The major source is probably Wells (1982), though that is occasionally a little out of date now. On comparing varieties see McMahon (2002: chapter 8).

7 The revenge of the colonised

As we have already seen, as soon as English speakers left Britain, they started to meet various kinds of entities and actions which were not familiar to them, and to borrow or coin words for these things. These words became part of the colonial Englishes, but they also became, by the same token, part of English. So while we may want to say that *kangaroo* is a word of Australian English, or *racoon* is word of North American English, they are also the English words for these animals, and can be used in Ireland and South Africa just as well as in Australia and Canada.

Many such words of this type were returned to Britain, and became part of standard British English, not only from the inner circle countries, but also from countries where English was the medium of administration or where English was a foreign language. Some examples, a few of which may be surprising, are given in Figure 7.1.

It is quite clear that as trade and exploration reported back new discoveries, new words to describe these discoveries would become part of general English. The English language seems to have a tradition of welcoming such words from all quarters. The frequency of mention of some languages in the etymology sections of *The Oxford English Dictionary* is given in Figure 7.2. (These counts are not straightforward to interpret. Some words may be derived from one or more of several languages, such as *baksheesh* which may be either Turkish or Urdu; some mentions may be mentions of cognates rather than mentions of origins; some mentions may even be denials of connection, such as the mention of 'Welsh' at *bachelor* which specifically denies any connection with Welsh *bach*; some languages are also mentioned in abbreviated forms, and these have not been included in the count; and some mentions may be cited words rather than indicators of origin. Nevertheless, such a list provides some clues as to the frequency of foreign words from the cited languages in English.) This is intended as a rough guide to the kinds of languages from which English has borrowed most extensively.

English word	Borrowed from
chintz	Hindi
ketchup	Chinese (Cantonese)
kiosk	Turkish
shampoo	Hindi
shawl	Persian
sofa	Arabic
tank	Gujerati or Marathi
tattoo	Marquesan
tea	Chinese

Figure 7.1 Some words returned to Britain by overseas trade

Language	Number of mentions
Arabic	181
Aztec	15
Chinese (some 'dialects' are also mentioned individually)	286
Hawaiian	65
Hindi (Hindustani is also mentioned)	447
Pawnee	1
Tibetan	38
Turkish	162
Urdu	223

Figure 7.2 Number of mentions of various languages in the etymology sections of *The Oxford English Dictionary*

The influence of the erstwhile British Empire and world trade on Britain has been not only in vocabulary, but also in customs: 'British cuisine' today is as likely to be curry as roast beef. I was told recently by a visitor to Britain that they had noted, and found striking, a half-timbered house with a sign outside reading 'Ye Olde Tudor Tandoori House': the house may have been Tudor, but the Tudors never ate Tandoori meals.

While all this has introduced a number of words with irregular spelling patterns into English, and has changed the density of Germanic words in English, there is a sense in which these changes are not particularly surprising, and have not changed the fundamental structure of the language at all. More interesting are those cases where the language systems in the colonies have had an effect on the language system in Britain, or where the words and phrases which have been borrowed back into British English are not obviously foreign in their nature.

7.1 Vocabulary

Have you been to the movies recently, or eaten a cookie, or had run-in with a bouncer at a night-club? If so, and you are American, this is scarcely surprising: *movie, cookie, bouncer* are all words of American origin. But if you are British then you have been the victim of colonial revenge in that you have adopted colonial vocabulary.

Attitudes to such Americanisms in Britain have been of some interest in themselves. Originally, many of them were not understood. Strang (1970: 37) lists some words of British English that American servicemen in Britain in the Second World War (1939–45) could not understand, and in many cases it seems likely that the British would not have understood the corresponding American term. A similar publication was published for New Zealand in 1944. Among the Americanisms that non-Americans were not expected to be familiar with at the period are: *bingo, bouncer, commuter,* (ice cream) *cone, elevator, hardware, porterhouse* (steak), *radio, raincoat, soft drink, truck.* The British English equivalents are, respectively, *housey (housey), chucker-out, season-ticket holder, cornet, lift, ironmongery, sirloin, wireless, mackintosh, mineral (water), lorry.*

Subsequent attitudes have swung between extreme anti-Americanism and extreme pro-Americanism (the former often on the expressed grounds of 'ruining the language', the latter often on the grounds that American expressions are 'colourful'). Both sides of the argument have been marred by failure to recognise a genuine Americanism. Many Americanisms (like those listed above) have slipped in unnoticed; many other expressions have been mistakenly taken to be Americanisms. Some examples of Americanisms are given in Figure 7.3: those in the first column were known in Britain by 1935, the second column presents some rather more recent Atlantic travellers.

No other variety has had as much influence of the language of 'home' as US English both because of the number of speakers and because of its use in the media. Few native English speakers around the world will go a day without hearing or reading some American English these days. However, there is some slight evidence of Australianisms also being used in Britain, such as *plonk* for cheap wine and *yachtie* for yachtsman/yachtswoman.

7.2 Grammar

The strongest grammatical influence by any colonial variety of English on the home variety comes from North American English, for the reasons outlined in the previous section. Even with British and American varieties of English, it is hard to be absolutely sure that changes that

cereal (for breakfast)	appendicitis
crook ('criminal')	disc jockey
footwear	draftee
get a move on	hospitalise
get away with	racketeer
high-brow	rat race
iron out	soap opera
jay-walker	usherette
joy-ride	
rough-house	
snow under	

Figure 7.3 Some Americanisms

make the two more similar actually arise from direct influence of the one on the other. An alternative hypothesis is that English is gradually changing, but that it is changing more rapidly in some varieties than in others. According to this hypothesis (for which see Hundt 1998), where we find British English adopting patterns which have been standard for some time in North America, this might be because the British varieties are just making the same changes rather more slowly, and not because British varieties are copying North American ones at all. Crucial evidence is hard to come by. To prove copying we would like to see evidence that a feature which has always been present in American English had died out in British English and has subsequently been re-suscitated. Such evidence is rarely available, if only because relevant features tend to persist in some if not all regional dialects, and there is always the possibility of interference between dialects. This will have to be borne in mind in evaluating the examples below.

In English, the verb in the present tense (and in the past tense with the verb to *be*), agrees in number with the subject of the sentence. Thus we find the typical situation in (1) and (2), where (1) has a singular subject and a singular -*s* on the verb, and (2) has a plural subject and no marking on the verb. (3) and (4) illustrate the past tense of *be*.

(1) The mouse eats the cheese.
(2) The mice eat the cheese.
(3) The mouse was small.
(4) The mice were small.

Nouns such as *class, committee, government* or *team* cause a problem when they act as subjects, though. Such nouns are termed 'collective nouns'. Are they singular and so required to take singular marking on the verb (after all, *classes, committees,* etc. would be their obvious plural forms and demand plural concord), or are they plural because a class is made up of a number of individuals who together form the class, and so on? The result of the uncertainty is that, for several centuries, there has been variation in English between constructions like those in (5) and (6):

(5) The committee has decided to approve the project.
(6) The committee have decided to approve the project.

In the course of the twentieth century, at least in certain types of writing, there has been an increase in the use of singular concord (as in (5)) in such cases in British English, though the trend has not been the same with every collective noun (Bauer 1994b: 63–6). This is widely assumed to arise through the influence of American English, where the singular is the norm in formal, edited writing. This is one of those cases that is hard to prove, since variation between the two forms has persisted at all times in British English (see for example Visser 1963: §77), and we could just be seeing a process of gradual drift.

The next example may be slightly clearer. It is the use of *not* and an unmarked verb after certain verbs such as *suggest*. In current English, (7) is generally accepted, while (8) is an alternative possibility.

(7) It was suggested that he not write the letter.
(8) It was suggested that he should not write the letter.

According to Visser (1963: §871), the construction in (7) probably originated in North America, and at the time of the settlement of North America the usual type was still to have the verb and the *not* the other way round, as in (9), from Shakespeare's *Troilus and Cressida*:

(9) 'Tis meet Achilles meet not Hector.

Visser cites examples of the pattern in (9) from as late as the 1940s, even in American writings. Although it is not clear precisely when the construction in (7) was first used (it may have been in the twentieth century), it has passed from being a purely American form to being also a British one. While the history of this particular construction is rather obscure, it does seem to be one minor case where the syntax of a colonial variety has triumphed over the home construction.

7.3 Pronunciation

Many people seem to believe that people will pick up American or Australian accents through watching American or Australian TV shows (Chambers 1998). They therefore expect people who grow up in Britain or New Zealand or South Africa to display features of these accents. But there is very little hard evidence that people are affected in this way. Certainly, individual words and phrases are picked up from such programmes: *sufferin' succotash* from Sylvester, *cowabunga!* from the Teenage Mutant Ninja Turtles, *Oh my God! they've killed Kenny!* from Southpark. Such expressions did not need the broadcast media to catch on, as is shown by Damon Runyon's *more than somewhat* from 1930, which started as a joke and rapidly became a standard expression. These individual words may be pronounced mimicking the accent in which they have been heard, in the same way that British listeners mimic other British accents when quoting the Goon Show ('he's fallen in the water!') or Monty Python's Flying Circus ('luxury!', 'Nobody expects the Spanish Inquisition'). But this does not mean that people adopt such accents wholesale any more than it means that people speak (or spoke) like Bluebottle (from the Goon Show) all the time.

Accordingly, it is a rare case if it can be shown that a feature of pronunciation has actually been adopted in British English from colonial varieties. This is all the more difficult since most features of pronunciation which are found in colonial varieties and become typical of those varieties started off as features of some form of British English.

This is even true of such well-worn examples as *lieutenant* and *schedule*. Here the standard US pronunciations are /luːtɛnənt/ and /skɛdjuːl/ respectively, and the conservative British pronunciations are /lɛftɛnənt/ and /ʃɛdjuːl/, respectively. The situation in most places outside the USA (and this specifically includes Canada) is some kind of mixture of the two, with the standard US pronunciations likely to take over completely in the future. In the eighteenth century the pronunciation for *lieutenant* was /lɛvtɛnənt/, although /l(j)uːtɛnənt/ was recognised as 'more regular'. Until late in the eighteenth century, the normal pronunciation for *schedule* was /sɛdjuːl/, and both /skɛdjuːl/ and /ʃɛdjuːl/ seem to be late eighteenth- and early nineteenth-century innovations (see *The Oxford English Dictionary*). The pronunciation with /ʃ/ is said to be a French pronunciation (although the corresponding French word has [s] and not [ʃ]), while the /sk/ pronunciation is used on the grounds that the word is of Greek origin. The point with these examples is that even pronunciation differences which, in the middle of the twentieth century, would have looked like clear discrepancies between British and American norms, turn out to have a more complicated history than this view allows for.

Because examples like *lieutenant* and *schedule* are the norm, the following case is one of some interest, but at the same time a controversial one.

In some varieties of English, there is a distinctive intonation pattern known in technical circles as the 'High Rise Terminal' or HRT. The

HRT consists of a rising intonation pattern on something that functions as a statement. People who are not used to varieties with HRT think that speakers who use them are asking questions all the time or are very insecure about what they are saying. Speakers who use them are quite aware that they are not asking questions and feel totally secure; they may, however, be checking that the interlocutor is following the exposition, especially at a particularly important point in a narrative. Students who use HRTs will go to see their lecturers and say 'Hi! I'm Kim Brown? I'm in your English course?' (the question marks indicate the rising intonation, and the effect such discourse has on people who are used to different varieties).

HRTs are commented on in print for New Zealand English in the early 1960s (Bauer 1994a: 396). The same or a very similar phenomenon drew comment in Australian English in 1965 (Turner 1994: 297). There is published comment on the phenomenon in the United States from the early 1980s (Ching 1982), which cites reports of HRTs from the 1960s. And there is a detailed phonetic description of HRTs in Toronto English from the late 1980s (James *et al.* 1989). Although we don't know when they started, HRTs have even been reported from Falkland Islands English (Sudbury 2001). Finally, Mrs Mills' Style column in the English *Sunday Times* for 7 January 2001 deals with the following question:

> Have you noticed this new accent hanging around Londoners these days, even amidst the Queen's English-speaking subjects? That of speaking questioningly, or is it only me who has? For example: 'I was late because I had to wait for the bus?' or 'It was getting quite late? So I thought I'd e-mail him instead?' Where has it come from and how come I am about the only person to notice?

Precisely how HRTs have developed in English is obscure. It is not clear where they first arose, nor whether their development in so many different varieties is independent or not, nor why they have not so far been adopted in South African English. What does seem to be true, is that the HRT developed in the colonies, and appeared in Britain after it was well established elsewhere. As such, it is a candidate for the first major and demonstrable phonetic effect to go from the colonies to Britain rather than vice versa.

7.4 Conclusion

One of the interesting, but puzzling, things about the revenge of the colonists is just how upset it makes people. Crystal (1997: 117) puts the feeling of threat in the face of Americanisms down to the sheer number of American users of English. This certainly explains the relative strength of American influences and influences from other parts of the world: if each part of the world had an influence proportional to the number of speakers of English found there, the influence of the USA would be thirteen times that of Australia and between sixty and seventy times that of New Zealand or South Africa. But even that does not explain the sense of xenophobia that has, at least in the past, attached to the thought of American influence, as opposed to influence from other parts of the globe. History might explain British and Canadian negative reactions to perceived Americanisms, but negative reactions from elsewhere would seem to require some kind of sociological explanation.

That there are equally negative reactions to things perceived to be Americanisms from other parts of the world is absolutely clear. Consider the following case from Australia, for example. The website <http://www.publicdebate.com.au/is/617/> asks whether Americanisms are ruining Australia's language. When I visited the site on 27 August 2001, the answers were running at 67 per cent 'yes' and only 4 per cent 'don't care'. And this is only revenge at one remove – Australia and the USA are parallel in the way they have taken the English language and made it their own. Any issue that gets this kind of response is clearly touching on something that people feel strongly about. Yet there is no immediate threat, and Americanisms have been used in the rest of the world for about 200 years without the English we speak becoming incomprehensible or invalid. Some people recognise this, and not only fail to understand the negative attitudes mentioned above, they find Americanisms positively attractive, indicative of being up-to-date and in fashion. At the same time, we have seen that many Americanisms are not recognised as such, and are used perfectly happily by everybody. And it is only a subset of American pronunciations which come in for criticism: /təˈmeɪtoː/ may be found amusing or odd; /raʊt/ for *route* is found definitely strange by everyone except computer programmers; but /bɑːks/ for *box* is scarcely commented on.

Exercises

1. As a class exercise, go and talk to people and ask them about Americanisms in the English language. Ask them for examples of Americanisms, as well as for their attitude towards them. After you have talked to the people, check whether the things they say are Americanisms really are. How will you do this? If you can find evidence of people's reactions to Americanisms from 'Letters to the Editor' columns, look at the arguments that are presented either for or against

Americanisms. How do you react to these arguments? How do your consultants react to them?

2. The use of the so-called subjunctive after verbs of suggesting, requiring and ordering is a feature which is more frequent in American English than in British English, and which is generally believed to be increasing in British English, especially in formal contexts (see section 4.2.1). Thus (i) used to be American English, but might now also be British English, while (ii) is more likely to be British English.

(i)   The university required that she complete the course.
(ii) The university required that she should complete the course.

Strang (1970: 58) presents a slightly sceptical view, suggesting that the contexts in which sentences like (i) and (ii) might be used may be becoming more frequent in British English, rather than use of the construction changing. How would you go about trying to decide whether (a) the use of the construction in British English is actually increasing and (b) whether this is due to the influence of American English? The construction is discussed in Visser (1963: §870) (though the terminology there is different). Visser does not solve the problem, but provides some indicators as to the timing.

3. Make a list of American and British translations (some have already been given in earlier chapters).

4. Take ten of the pairs you have listed in response to question 3 where both the terms are in use in your community. Either by looking at actual texts or by asking people's opinions, see if you can determine who uses which word and why.

Recommendations for reading

Go online to read Sussex (1999) on Americanisms in Australian English or see Peters (2001).

8 Becoming independent

We can be sure that with the Declaration of American Independence in 1776, and the War of Independence which went on for several years beyond that, those whose families had fought the British in an attempt to gain independence had no great feeling of being the same as the British any more. It must have been very easy for them, then, to have felt that they were, as a group, distinct enough from the British, not only to have their own country, but also to have their own language. And it is not long before we start finding references to an American language. As early as 1783, we find Noah Webster advocating a 'national language' for America, and by 1789 he was referring to this national language as 'the American tongue' (cited in McArthur 1998: 220). By 1800 works were appearing with the title 'the American language', and by 1802 'American' was being contrasted with 'English', referring to two varieties of language clearly viewed as distinct (see citations in McArthur 1998 and the *The Oxford English Dictionary*). This is a complete change from usage in the seventeenth century when the term 'American language' was used of the language(s) of the native peoples of North America. By 1923, the state of Illinois could decree that its official language should be known as 'the American language' and not 'the English language' (cited in McArthur 1998: 221). The use of 'American' to refer to the English spoken in America continues to the present day, though frequently with less positive connotations than Webster would have wished, particularly from British writers (see sections 7.1, 7.4 and discussion of the exercises for Chapter 7). In 1993, the American columnist William Safire wrote '*With unmistakable disdain,* the broadcastocrats in London call what we speak "American"' (cited in McArthur 1998; my italics). However, the term is not always viewed negatively: a brief search of the World-Wide Web shows that many US universities have an 'American language program' in which English as a second or foreign language is taught. While these are advertised under an 'American' title, the explanation is virtually always in terms of the teaching of 'English language'. There is thus some tension between the two terms, with 'English' apparently being more explanatory, but 'American' viewed as being more attractive, at least within the USA, and possibly also in the countries which provide the customers for such courses.

In the other countries where inner circle varieties of English are spoken, there was not the same break with the Home variety, nor the same reaction against things British. Accordingly, there was not the same rejection of British norms. Indeed, the opposite was the case. In both Australia and New Zealand this has been termed the 'cultural cringe', the phenomenon whereby overseas, especially European, cultural achievements (including British cultural achievements) are seen as being far more worthy and valuable than those in the colony, with a corresponding denigration of colonial norms. The term was apparently first used in 1950 (Ramson 1988), which indicates the period at which this assumption started to be queried: before that time, it was simply a norm and no term was needed. Not only were Antipodean writers, artists and musicians automatically considered inferior to their British peers (at least until they had achieved recognition in Britain or Europe), colonial forms of the English language were automatically viewed as inferior to a British prestige variety. It follows that though Australasian vocabulary might have been considered amusing or quaint, there could be no Australasian standards which were accepted as such: the standards were British ones. This is not to say that there were no *de facto* local standards: there were. But these standards could not be overtly accepted as standards.

In this environment, it is scarcely surprising that early uses of 'Australian language' (meaning English) frequently indicate an over-use of slang terms, swearwords and a broad accent. 'New Zealand' is rarely used in the same way that 'American' is to denote the language: the language can, though, be 'New Zild' (indicating the clipped pronunciation of 'New Zealand' in a broad New Zealand accent). 'South African' or 'Canadian' are scarcely used as words denoting varieties of English (though the terms 'South African English' and 'Canadian English' are widely used).

The notion of standard in language is notoriously difficult to pin down. Although many people would claim to be able to recognise a standard version of their own language, it is very difficult to provide a set of criteria which prove this to be a standard form. One criterion among others which is often cited, though, is codification: standard varieties are described in grammars, style manuals, dictionaries, pronunciation guides, and so on, while non-standard varieties are either ignored in such publications, treated in learned works on dialects and language variation, or treated (linguistically often very poorly) in light-hearted publications intended to amuse as much as instruct. We can see why this should be: it is a matter of publishing economics. Lay people want (and are willing to pay for) books which describe a variety of language which has high prestige and which they feel they should be imitating in their official writing; they are not willing to pay for descriptions of varieties which, if they were imitated, would lead only to disrepute. Thus economic argument masks a lack of perceived value in things which are not standard; accordingly, only descriptions of things seen as standard can be sold to large numbers of people, and so standard varieties of languages are much better documented than non-standard varieties. For our purposes in this book, this can be turned on its head: to the extent that a variety is codified in widely published materials, it is an indication that there is a perception of this variety as a standard.

Given what we have said, we would predict that codifications of American English would begin late in the eighteenth or early in the nineteenth century, but that codifications of other national varieties of English would follow considerably later, well into the twentieth century. This is basically what we find. We can discuss this codification in five strands: lexis or vocabulary (in dictionaries), grammar, pronunciation (in dictionaries and pronunciation dictionaries), style and, finally, discussions of the variety used in textbooks and the like. For American English there is the extra strand of orthography. In order to make sense of the colonial evidence, we also need to know what was happening in the home varieties, so we will start with British Englishes.

8.1 British Englishes

English dictionaries start in the sixteenth century. Thomas Cooper's translating dictionary, *Thesaurus Linguae Romanae et Britannicae*, was published in 1565. In his *Brief Lives* (Aubrey 1975: 79), John Aubrey tells the story of Cooper's wife being so incensed at the long hours he spent working on the dictionary that she threw it in the fire. But he just started again. Families of many other lexicographers have felt the same way.

Monolingual English dictionaries come later. Robert Cawdrey's *A Table Alphabeticall* of 1604 is generally assumed to be the first. It contains approximately 3000 'hard usuall English wordes, borrowed from the Hebrew, Greeke, Latine, or French &c', collected 'for the benefit & helpe of Ladies, Gentlewomen, or any other unskilfull persons' who might need to understand these words, 'which they shall heare or read in Scriptures, Sermons, or elsewhere'. It was not until the eighteenth century that the idea of providing a 'complete' list of English words first arose, or of providing etymologies for those words. It was against that background, and the background of the formation of Italian and French language academies, that Johnson's dictionary was written. Johnson did not want an Academy, but he did want a dictionary, to help the ignorant and to help 'fix' the language. In 1747 he wrote his plan of the dictionary, which was addressed to Lord Chesterfield, from whom he hoped for patronage. It was not forthcoming. So Johnson got the backing of some booksellers and set to work, with the help of a handful of amanuenses. His *Dictionary of the English Language* was published in 1755, only seven years later. It contains 43,500 words, illustrated with 118,000 citations from the best authors. At this point Lord Chesterfield suddenly decided that perhaps he should have been in on the act. No wonder the *Dictionary* definition of PATRON is

> One who countenances, supports or protects. Commonly a wretch who supports with insolence, and is paid with flattery.

In fact, the Dictionary is noted for its sometimes idiosyncratic definitions, such as

> OATS: A grain, which in England is generally given to horses, but in Scotland supports the people.

> LEXICOGRAPHER: a writer of dictionaries, a harmless drudge, that busies himself in tracing the original [*i.e. origin*], and detailing the signification of words.

The major dictionary of British English, originally commissioned by the Philological Society, was a late nineteenth-century project. It was begun in 1870, and published from 1884 onwards, under the title *A New English Dictionary on Historical Principles*. The dictionary was completed in 1928, and republished in 1933 in twelve volumes under the title of *The Oxford English Dictionary*.

The development of Scottish dictionaries ran very much in parallel with that of English ones. Following a number of glossaries, John Jamieson's *An Etymological Dictionary of the Scottish Language* was published starting in 1808, and the *Scottish National Dictionary*, which covers Scottish language from 1700 onwards was not completed until 1976, nearly seventy years after it had first been mooted.

Grammars of English were first written in the sixteenth century, and some, such as the one by playwright Ben Jonson (1640), were written in the seventeenth century. The major ones, however, were written in the eighteenth century, notably Robert Lowth's in 1762. Since then, there has been a flood of grammatical description, with several new grammatical descriptions of English still being worked on today.

English pronunciation became an issue once it had changed so much that the spelling was no longer seen as a guide to pronunciation. This implies a recognised standard of spelling, which was not established until well into the seventeenth century. The first important works listing pronunciations were published in the eighteenth century, including Thomas Sheridan's *General Dictionary of the English Language* (1780) and John Walker's *Critical Pronouncing Dictionary of the English Language* (1791).

The generalisation here is that English was not fully codified until the eighteenth century, when the prevailing philosophy of the day led people to wish to 'fix' or 'ascertain' what was correct English. By the time the United States had become an independent nation there was, therefore, a tradition of codifying English, and a base to build on.

8.2 North American Englishes

Amongst many other things (American patriot, soldier, lawyer, school-teacher, editor, lexicographer), Noah Webster (1758–1843) was an advo-cate of spelling reform. In 1789 he published a work calling for a radical spelling reform, omitting unnecessary letters and making a number of simplifications. Most of these did not survive into his later works, but the American spellings illustrated in *color, center, defense* can be attributed directly to his work, and even the spelling *public* (which he insisted on as opposed to *publick* which was still common in England at the period), may be seen as one of his victories. Webster's *An American Dictionary of the English Language* (1828) and his *The American Spelling Book* (1783) were the most influential works in distinguishing British from American spelling conventions.

An American Dictionary of the English Language was also one of the first dictionaries to make a serious attempt to list new American meanings for old terms and to list new American words unknown in England. The dictionary is often criticised for not having listed many Americanisms (perhaps it was not clear at that period just what were Americanisms and whether or not they could be seen as part of the standard language), but Webster does list American meanings for words like *bluff, constitution, corn, creek, marshal, robin, sherif* (sic), while also mentioning British usages. He includes words such as *dime, dollar, hickory, moccason* (sic), *racoon, skunk, sleigh* and *wigwam*. He does not list *boss* ('master'), *canyon, coyote, poison ivy, prairie, teepee,* or *totem* (of these, only *canyon* may have been too new for a listing; the first citation in *The Oxford English Dictionary* is from 1837). Like Johnson, he lists *mocking bird* and *squash* ('a plant'). He uses the spellings *gray* and *traveler*, but also *maiz, melasses* and *trowsers* which have not persisted.

The first dictionary of Canadian words was not published until 1967:

A Dictionary of Canadianisms. Canadian words had previously been included in US dictionaries. Dictionaries considering the vocabulary of some of the provinces of Canada (Newfoundland, Prince Edward Island) followed in the 1980s. A *Guide to Canadian English Usage* was published in 1997.

The first American English grammar was, ironically, written in England – by Lindley Murray in 1795. What is more, Murray's grammar was used with equal success on both sides of the Atlantic. It was fairly conservative even when new, but continued to be used in schools for a century. Webster also included a grammar as part of his 1828 dictionary. Surprisingly, pronunciation dictionaries of American English are not published until much later. Pronunciation is first listed in ordinary dictionaries, and the major dictionary of US pronunciation was first published in 1944 (Kenyon and Knott 1953), overtly following a British model.

8.3 Southern hemisphere Englishes

The earliest dictionary of a southern hemisphere English, *A Dictionary of Austral English*, was published in 1898. *The Australian National Dictionary* wasn't published until 1988, 200 years after settlement. *The Australian National Dictionary* focuses on just those words which are peculiar to Australia, and is not a general English dictionary. There are several general English dictionaries published in Australia and for Australian users, of which the most notable is the *Macquarie Dictionary* (first edition 1981). Similar patterns are found in South Africa, with the dictionary called *Africanderisms* published in 1913, and The *Dictionary of South African English* published in 1996. New Zealand in many ways shares the *Dictionary of Austral English* with Australia, but has its own *Dictionary of New Zealand English*, published in 1997. In every case, the general dictionaries aimed at local southern hemisphere markets started to appear in the late 1970s.

There are no specific grammars of southern hemisphere Englishes; it is still assumed that what is true of British English (and, perhaps increasingly, of American English) is true of these other varieties. We know that this is not the case (see Chapter 4), but as yet the differences are not so great as to make the writing of a separate grammar a commercial concern. The same is true of pronunciation. Many of the general dictionaries for local consumption give transcriptions of the words listed, but the transcriptions provided could, on the whole, just as well be transcriptions of RP. This is not quite true: the *New Zealand Pocket Oxford Dictionary* (second edition 1997) makes no distinction between the unstressed vowels in *gibbon* and *gibbet*, and marks the first syllable of *geyser* as rhyming with *guy*; but it makes no mention of any possible pronunciation of *assume* other than /əsjuːm/, despite the frequent appearance of /əʃuːm/ and /əsuːm/. Perhaps it is fairer to say that pronunciations indicated in such works are, by default, equivalent to RP, but may vary where the colony concerned uses a phonemically distinct form either universally or clearly as a majority form in maximally precise speech. This has the effect of making transcriptions look more similar than the pronunciations they are intended to represent would warrant.

Interestingly, despite the lack of grammars, there are southern hemisphere style manuals, notably *The Cambridge Australian Style Guide* (1995). Unlike the *Chicago Manual of Style*, this is not simply a book on how to present material on a printed page, but gives a great deal of information and advice on near homophones, spelling variants and grammatical information, like Fee and McAlpine (1997) on Canadian English. It is very like Fowler's (1965) *Modern English Usage*, but with an Australian slant.

8.4 Discussion

English was well codified by the time of the Declaration of Independence, and because of the political situation in which Americans found themselves at the time, it was felt to be expedient to codify American English as different from British English virtually immediately after the War of Independence. Because the political situation was not as fraught in the case of southern hemisphere varieties of English, there was a greater temptation to see local varieties of English simply as corrupted versions of British English, with Britain providing the standard variety. Accordingly, there was far less political pressure for South African and Australasian varieties of English to be seen as independent, and the codification of these varieties has taken longer. Even today, the attitude that colonial Englishes are 'slovenly' or 'lazy' and lack prestige still finds occasional expression, although such views are not now expressed as often as they were as recently as the 1970s. The New Zealand author, Dame Ngaio Marsh, called New Zealand English 'the ugliest dialect in the world', while others said that New Zealand children's accents sounded like 'a linen draper's assistant tearing a sheet of unbleached calico'; nowadays, even the radio stations say that 'we like New Zealanders who are speaking to New Zealanders to sound like New Zealanders' (all cited in Blundell 2001). Similar changes of attitudes could be found for all of the colonial Englishes, with slight differences in actual timing.

At the same time, if we expect full grammars and pronunciation lists for all these varieties, we will have a long time to wait. Until recently, such things have not been viable as commercial publication ventures, and it seems unlikely that a grammar of a variety such as South African English (with relatively few native speakers, though there are many non-native speakers) will, in the near future, get a fully independent grammar – though it could get a South African addendum to an established grammar of some larger variety. The differences are not yet great enough, nor the number of potential users large enough, to make an independent work a realistic option in the short term.

8.5 The break-up of English?

Given that there are now significant differences between the Englishes spoken in England and in other parts of the world, it is timely to consider the likelihood that these will move so far apart that it will eventually no longer be appropriate to consider them as varieties of the same language. If we look back into European history, we have an apparent precedent in the case of Latin. Latin changed so much in the course of a millennium that it was no longer called 'Latin' in the places where it was used, and the various 'dialects' of Latin became so different that speakers of one could not understand speakers of another. Today we don't talk about people speaking modern Latin in Europe, but about them speaking French, Italian, Portuguese, Spanish, Romanian and so on. Perhaps in another few hundred years, we will similarly say that people talk 'American', 'Australian' and 'South African' instead of saying that they talk English.

Many people believe that it is inevitable. Everything we know about language history up to the middle of the last century suggests that varieties of any language diverge when left to themselves, they do not converge. And where pronunciation is concerned, there is ample evidence that local varieties of English continue to diverge. It is not hard to find local varieties of English which are incomprehensible to outsiders who have no experience of listening to them. Change is affecting the vowels of US English very rapidly in some areas. In the so-called 'northern cities shift', which affects speakers in cities such as Detroit, the vowel in *bat* has become closer that the vowel in *bet* (and thus rather more like the vowel in *bit*) in the course of a single generation (Labov 1994: 99–100). This is a major disturbance to the English vowel system, and one which can prevent people from further south or west in the USA from understanding those from Detroit. Other major changes within living memory have affected the TRAP vowel in RP, the KIT vowel in New

Zealand English, and so on. These are the kinds of changes that led to French being different from Italian and Spanish.

McArthur (1998) argues passionately that a monolithic view of English as 'a' language is no longer sufficient to cope with the reality we meet from people all round the world who say that they speak 'English' (and, indeed, in some cases this is their only language). McArthur bases his view, though, on a rather wider sample than has been considered in this book: he considers Jamaican patois and the Tok Pisin of Papua New Guinea alongside the English used daily in India, the Philippines, Singapore and elsewhere. The 'Englishes' he views are far more different than the Englishes we have looked at here. But the general principle is the same: people do not all speak English the same way, and there is evidence of increasing disparity between the different types of language they all call 'English'. This book has focussed on the differences: their sources, the problems of description they give rise to, and so on.

So is English inevitably going to splinter into a large number of mutually incomprehensible languages? If we consider all the types considered by McArthur, then I believe that the answer is 'yes'. However, if we look at just those inner circle varieties which have been the main focus of this book, there are some factors which suggest that the irrevocable split may not yet have occurred.

First, we do not yet know what role the media will play in the future of English. Films and television may not make us all sound American (Chambers 1998), but they do make us used to listening to Americans and Australians, even if we do not have personal contact with many people from those countries. Accordingly, other Englishes are probably less foreign to us now than they were to our (great-)grandparents in the 1940s. Whether or not we say *Did you eat yet?* we recognise the structure and know what it means.

Then we have the rather unexpected finding that there is in recent times some evidence of language convergence rather than divergence. In some cases we even have a name for the phenomenon: 'mid-Atlantic' or 'mid-Pacific'. The evidence comes from places like Tyneside in England (Watt and Milroy 1999) where very local regional features seem to be disappearing in favour of some form of regional English, perhaps a general north of England English. This form of accent levelling is in principle the same as the accent levelling we have already met operating in colonial situations; the difference is that there is not mobility from one country to another, but mobility from a number of rural areas into the main cities, and then between the main cities.

And we must distinguish between what is happening in the written language and what is happening in the spoken language. Even if the spoken language is diverging, the formal written language shows (as yet) little evidence of such divergence. Indeed, one of the many advantages claimed for English is that you can sit down and read a work written in Canada or Australia or Tyneside wherever in the English-speaking world you come from. The differences of grammar between varieties are (as we have seen in Chapter 4) very slight. Latin as a written language lasted virtually into the seventeenth century in Europe, and it could be that English as a written language will outlast spoken English as an international medium of communication. Another possibility, though, is that international communication will remain a powerful enough force to prevent varieties of English diverging too far from each other, and thus slow down (if not prevent) the divergent pressures.

One thing remains certain: prediction is a very uncertain business. We can see the forces massed to cause the break-up of English, and we can see the centripetal forces which might attempt to withstand that attack. Precisely what the outcome will be and over what period is impossible to predict. An overwhelming change in global politics could disrupt the system so much that all our predictions could become invalid. But we will not be around in 500 years to see how our predictions have fared; we can only hope that historians of that future time will be understanding of our inability to guess how things would turn out and why.

Exercises

1. Draw a time line showing settlement, independence and markers of independent language (such as the first local dictionaries) for the various colonies discussed in this book. Discuss what it shows.

2. The following is taken from a letter to the editor of the *New Zealand Listener*:

> The fact is that American English has evolved into a form that is different from British English both in vocabulary and pronunciation, but which is perfectly acceptable. There is, however, precious little New Zealand English worth recording. Most of it is sheer misuse and mispronunciation of British English.

Why does the writer see American English as a separate variety but New Zealand English as a corrupt variety of British English? What would you see as the major difference between the two? This letter appeared in 1983; what do you think this tells you about the writer?

3. Here is another letter from a local newspaper, *Contact*, in Wellington, New Zealand, but some nine years later.

I'm sorry, I can't take harassment any longer. That is to say, I cannot take it pronounced harris-ment.

It is true that I do know some men called Harris with a twinkle in their eye. But it has nothing to do with them.

It is pronounced appropriately enough *her-assment*. Almost all newsreaders get the pronunciation of this word wrong.

Why does this letter show a contrast with the last? Why would news-readers, of all people, be likely to use the pronunciation the writer considers 'wrong'? How would you answer the writer?

4. The following passage comes from the South African newspaper *Mail and Guardian* (2–8 February 2001, p. 13).

Health authorities may try to curtail or even outlaw the annual Swazi *bacchanal* that commences with the arrival of *buganu*, the traditional brew fermented from the fruit of the maganu tree.

But even in the light of a cholera outbreak that may be worsened by a brew made from tainted water, the summertime overindulgence that inspires legendary public sexual escapades is not likely to be inhibited.

'Nobody is going to stop the *buganu* from flowing,' says Sipho Matsebula, a bus conductor whose shoulders bulk up at this time of year as he hefts large drums of the country brew to the tops of long-haul buses for delivery to urban centres, including Johannesburg.

What makes this a South African text? Can you distinguish between the setting that the text discusses and the language in which the text is written? How would you have to change this text to avoid it being a South African text?

Recommendations for reading

On the split of English, McArthur (1998) makes very interesting reading. For a contrasting view, see Quirk (1985).

9   Standards in the colonies

Wherever we go in the world, we find a number of different varieties of English, the features of which are not determined by whether we are in Canada or Australia but by how formally we are writing or talking and by who we are. An invented sentence like that in (1) could in principle arise in most places in the English-speaking world, with exactly the same features. It is not regional, but it shows a kind of variation which occurs within all the regional varieties.

(1)   This man come into the bar last night and he said all them things are wrong.

So far we have been making the pretence that there is just one level of language, both in Britain and in the colonies, a level which we can term a standard. It is the standard variety which is codified in the works discussed in Chapter 8. But as well as variation in the standard from country to country, there is variation away from the standard in each of the countries. The problem is to distinguish the two.

9.1 Moving away from the standard in vocabulary

The obvious examples of non-standard words are swear-words and other instances of 'bad language'. The most taboo of these words rarely make it into print in newspapers and magazines, though may appear in fiction, drama and poetry. But there is also another level of language which is not subject to taboos, and yet is still not regarded as 'good English'. Some expressions in this category, such as *stuff up* 'to make a mistake' are recently taboo words, but others such as *duff up* 'beat up' are not. Such words are usually termed slang words. We cannot predict whether slang is regionally restricted: some is, some is not. In a recent research programme in which eleven- and twelve-year-old New Zealand children were asked about the words they used to describe various things, we were given 168 different ways of saying that somebody told you off. These

growled me	threw/chucked/had/packed a spaz at me
bit/blew my head off	threw/went/had a psych at me
fell out of his tree	threw a (hissy) fit at me
freaked out	wasted me
gave me a blasting	went ape at me
greened out at me	went ape-o/hyp-o/spaz-o
lost his chill pills	went ballistic
packed/had/threw a fit at me	went mental at me
slagged me off	went off his block
stressed out at me	went shitty at me

Figure 9.1 New Zealand expressions for 'told me off'

bomb-ass	really good	dog on (a person)	make fun of
bootie	ugly, repulsive	earl	to vomit
buff	very muscular	flip a bitch	do a U-turn
crispy	pretentious	gleek	spit copiously
diesel	tough	hooride	car

Figure 9.2 Some American slang expressions from Munro (1997)

included all the expressions in Figure 9.1. Of these, we know that *growl somebody* is a local New Zealand expression, but we suspect that all the others can be found elsewhere. Unfortunately, this can be hard to prove, partly because slang words can be very ephemeral, and partly because many dictionaries do not include a lot of these slang words and expressions, and it can be difficult to discover how widespread they really are. The other side of the coin is provided by the words in Figure 9.2 from Munro (1997). These are slang words from California university students which still sound unfamiliar to me, and are thus probably locally American. (I could, of course, be wrong.)

As well as obvious slang terms, there are words which are used in particular registers only (such as when talking to children – words like *tootsies* for 'feet') which could be seen as non-standard but not necessarily regionalised words.

9.2 Moving away from the standard in grammar

There are a large number of features which are found in many international varieties of English and which are probably not viewed as completely standard in any of them. Some examples are provided below. What is interesting about these features is not whether they exist or not, but when and where they are used: are they restricted to conversation or are they used in formal speeches, in courts of law and in formal broadcasts?

A typical case is provided by invariable *there's*. Standard usage everywhere permits the pattern seen in (2) with *there is* for a single object and *there are* for several.

(2) There is a strange dog in the garden.
      There are some strange dogs in the garden.

However, *there's* is commonly used in both situations, especially in spoken English, but also in written English. Evans and Evans (1957), Peters (1995), Burchfield (1996) and Fee and McAlpine (1997) all imply that this is an informal construction, though the precise relationship between informal and non-standard is not clear.

Another is the use of *never* as a simple negator. In the standard English of England, there is a distinction to be made between (3) and (4).

(3) I didn't see John F. Kennedy trip.
(4) I never saw John F. Kennedy trip.

(3) refers to a single occasion, while (4) is a general statement more or less equivalent to 'on all the occasions on which I saw John F. Kennedy, I did not see him trip'. However, in Scottish English, *never* is used perfectly naturally to negate the single event, so that (4) can mean the same thing as (3) and we can hear things like

(5) I never watched *Friends* yesterday.

This same usage is found in Falkland Island English (Sudbury 2001: 73), New Zealand English, and South African English (Branford 1994: 491), and in other varieties as well, including North American ones. It is used in more formal contexts in Scotland than in these other varieties. Burchfield (1996) notes this usage but does not condemn it; Peters (1995) and Fee and McAlpine (1997) do not even mention it; this may suggest that it is on the way to being considered standard everywhere.

Another example which may have its origins in Scottish English is the use of *may* for *might*. A news broadcast on Radio New Zealand's prestigious National Radio in 1990 announced

(6) Some of the road deaths in the Auckland area may have been prevented if more staff had been available.

The road deaths had not been avoided. This construction is found in British English and in US English, but is clearly non-standard in both. In Australian (Newbrook 2001: 122) and New Zealand English the construction is rare, but less obviously non-standard in that it is used in the press and broadcasting quite freely.

There are some non-standard tags, too. In Australian, New Zealand and Falkland Islands English, *but* is found used as a tag, as in (7) (Turner 1994: 303, Sudbury 2001: 73).

(7) Funny old bag. I quite like her but.

There are two noun phrase constructions whose degree of standardness is changing rapidly at the present time. The first is usually illustrated with the phrase *between you and I*. The rule for English used to be that you used *you and I* in the places where you would use *I* alone, and *you and me* in the places where you would use *me* alone. Thus *You and I know better* (because it is *I know better* not **Me know better*), *He showed it to you and me* (because it is *He showed it to me*, not **He showed it to I*) and *They saw you and me last night* (because it is *They saw me*, not **They saw I*). The problem started when people used *me and him* (and other similar forms) in subject position: *Me and him were late*. Such utterances were corrected so often to forms with *I*, that the point of the correction was lost, and people began to believe that only *I* and never *me* could occur in co-ordinated phrases. My experience is that undergraduate students now believe that *He saw you and I* is better or more formal English than *He saw you and me*, and this observation is supported by Collins (1989: 146) for Australian English. This is an unexpected off-shoot of overt prescription. Meanwhile, there are still people (like me) who work with the old system, but even we are becoming contaminated by modern usage. This kind of variation is found everywhere that English is spoken as a native language, and it seems likely that in another fifty years or so the *between you and I* people will win out completely.

Another distinction that is disappearing in noun phrases is that between *less* and *fewer*. The difference used to be one of countability, parallel to the difference between *much* and *many* (see Quirk *et al.* 1985: 245–52). So where you could say *Much bread/knowledge/water* you could also say *Less bread/knowledge/water*, but where *many* was required as in *Many books/loaves/people* (not **Much books/loaves/people*) you had also to use *fewer*. For many speakers today, however, *Less books/loaves/people* is just as ordinary as the traditional *Fewer books/loaves/people*. A few years ago, a poster advertising a local radio station with the slogan 'More music, less commercials' was defaced by a literate graffiti artist with the words 'Fewer grammar'. In another few years, it seems unlikely that anyone will recognise a problem here. The same failure to maintain a count/non-count distinction is giving rise to the increasingly common phrase *a large amount of people*. Since *people* are countable (we can have *many people* but not *much people), traditionalists require *a large number of people: amount of* goes with the nouns that use *much*. Again, what was non-standard is becoming standard.

In some cases, like the *between you and I* one, self-appointed guardians of the language leap to prop up some usage which is going out of fashion and to decry an incoming usage. One such case is what you do with the adjective *different*. Which of the following is correct?

(8) It is different to what I'd expected.
     It is different from what I'd expected.
     It is different than what I'd expected.

You will probably find that you have quite firm ideas about which is 'correct', even if it is not the one you yourself use. These ideas are implanted by the prescriptions from the language guardians. There are arguments in favour of each of these, but they are spurious arguments. But because there is overt prescription, not only do we find people aware of the variation, we also find that prescriptions can differ from place to place. *Different to* is virtually unknown in the USA, but *different than* is much more common in formal writing in the USA than elsewhere (Hundt 1998: 105–8). *Different to* is found in Britain, in Australia and New Zealand mainly in informal contexts, while *different from* is the preferred formal version everywhere.

The examples given here are simply examples of a wider phenomenon – and, indeed, it might be argued that some of the grammatical features treated in Chapter 4 would have been better mentioned here instead. In all of these instances, a greater or lesser amount of variation may be tolerated in different varieties and the variation may be seen as closer to or further from the standard ideal. This makes the notion of standard very difficult to define: when I hear a Prime Minister of New Zealand saying in a broadcast interview

(9) It would have been better for New Zealand if the money had have been thrown off the Auckland Harbour Bridge.

is that a sign that the construction with *had have* (often written *had of*) has become standard in New Zealand English, or not, and how should I be able to determine this?

9.3 Moving away from the standard in pronunciation

People seem to have a fairly good picture of what a standard accent sounds like, and any divergence from that is seen as a move away from the standard. In particular, this applies to the use of rhoticity in Britain (and New Zealand) and to the lack of rhoticity in the USA, but it also applies to a host of quite minor differences such as quite slight differences in vowel quality (this is particularly true for the STRUT vowel and the GOAT vowel in British English). In addition there are a number of phenomena which mark a non-standard accent in most varieties of English.

- /h/-dropping: pronunciations such as /aʊs/ for *house*. (Note that /h/-dropping on unstressed words such as *him* in sentences like *Give him a biscuit* is perceived as being standard.)
- So-called <g>-dropping (although phonetically there is no [g] to be dropped): pronunciations such as /kʌmɪn/ for *coming*.
- The use of a final /k/ in words ending in *-thing* giving pronunciations such as /sʌmθɪŋk/.
- Loss of or reduction in use of /θ/ and /ð/. The situation with these sounds is complex and we do not need a detailed picture here. The fricative /θ/ in all positions and /ð/ in medial and final positions alternate with /f/ and /v/ respectively in urban British accents, under the influence of London (Cockney) English. This gives pronunciations like [fɪŋk] for *think* and [brʌvə] for *brother*. Such pronunciations are now occasionally heard in Australia and New Zealand. At the same time, /θ/ and /ð/ in all positions may be replaced by /t/ and /d/ respectively, under the influence of Hiberno-English and also older London English. This gives pronunciations like [tɪŋk] for *think* and [dɪs] for *this*. These are heard not only in Ireland and Liverpool, but also in some regional accents in the USA.
- Extensive use of a glottal stop either intervocalically or word finally: pronunciations like [bʌʔə] for *butter* and [kæʔ] for *cat*. (A certain amount of glottal use is compatible with standard status, as long as it is not intervocalic as in *butter*. In some varieties a tap is heard in such environments instead, giving [bʌɾə], and this may be considered standard, for example in Canada, the USA, Australia and New Zealand.)

Australian, New Zealand and South African varieties of English face another problem. Although each of these varieties is different from the others and different from Cockney, they all share certain pronunciation features with Cockney (probably because all four accents were caused by mixing other accents of relatively similar sorts). In a British context, Cockney is in some senses the non-standard accent *par excellence:* it is an accent of the capital city, and thus has no regional 'excuse' for being different from the prestige accent RP, it is simply a non-standard variety. In the colonial situation, accents which are reminiscent of Cockney have been tarred with the same brush. The opprobrium which is heaped upon Cockney (it is said, very unfairly, to be lazy, slovenly, ugly and so on) has been transferred to the colonial accents, in a way which has proved very difficult to avoid. As a result, these accents have been perceived as being non-standard accents of a foreign English and as we saw in Chapter 8 it is only recently that laypeople have started to perceive that there are standard and non-standard varieties of these colonial Englishes.

9.4 Discussion

There are two general points which arise from the material discussed here, one about the nature of standard in general, the other about the nature of what is non-standard.

Despite all the codification discussed in Chapter 7, it is not necessarily easy to say what is or is not standard in any particular variety of English. An extreme position might be that colonial varieties are, by their very nature, not standard varieties and that there is only one standard English, namely the standard English of southern England. An only slightly less extreme version of this would allow two standard forms, a British and a North American standard. This is the way in which Australian, New Zealand and South African Englishes have been viewed for a long time, although as we saw in Chapter 8 this is now changing.

If we wish to reject this extreme view, then we have to ask what it is that makes a particular variety of English standard in its own community. This usually involves factors such as being a variety used in formal broadcasting, a variety used in the judicial system, a variety used in higher education, sometimes a variety used in government and the church. The difficulty with such a definition is that when you actually examine the types of English used in these different environments, you discover that there is a great deal of variation within them. This then gives rise to another question: how much variation (if any) is ideally permissible within a standard variety? Such a question is not readily answerable, because it is not easily quantified. But what we can say is that standard varieties typically allow less variation than non-standard varieties (Milroy and Milroy 1985). Less variation is still not the same as no variation. Consider the variants in (10), for example, any one of which might be considered standard, though the first is now old-fashioned and if used at all is extremely formal.

(10)   The economist whom I met in Paris was a German.
       The economist who I met in Paris was a German.
       The economist that I met in Paris was a German.
       The economist I met in Paris was a German.

Even in the best-codified varieties, therefore, we are still left with problems of demarcation of the standard. For most purposes, it must be admitted, this does not matter at all. But if we want to talk about a standard Falkland Islands English or South African English, for example, we will need to know what that entails in order to delimit it successfully.

The second point is the nature of what is non-standard. In a place like Britain we can more or less equate regional with non-standard. For example, the term *mash* of tea is regionally limited and non-standard. The converse is not true: things which are non-standard are not necessarily narrowly regional. Consider rhoticity in Britain, which is found in over half of the British mainland – and probably in more than half of England (though not in the most prestigious accents), and is still not considered standard there. Cheshire *et al.* (1989) list a number of grammatical factors recognised by at least 85 per cent of their urban respondent schools, and these include:

- demonstrative *them*: *Look at them big spiders.*
- *should of*: *You should of left half an hour ago.*
- *never* as a past tense negator: *No, I never broke that.*
- *there was* with a plural: *There was some singers here.*

The fact that these are so widely recognised suggests that they are not narrow regionalisms, yet these are not standard forms. Other things like double negatives (*We don't have no money*) and adverbial use of adjectival forms (*He ran real quick*) have been suggested as factors which are more likely to be generally non-standard than markers of regionality (Cheshire *et al.* 1989: 194) – and while these two do show some regional variability within Britain, they are both widely found in colonial Englishes as well.

Once we start to consider colonial Englishes, we can no longer make the assumption that a narrowly regional form must be non-standard. This is perhaps most obvious with vocabulary items: very few people outside New Zealand are likely to know the words *boomer* and *borer*, but while *boomer* ('a whopper') is (dated) slang and rarely used in print, *borer* is an absolutely normal term for 'woodworm'. The same point is true, however, of features of grammar and pronunciation. The form *proven* is probably standard in Scotland and the USA, non-standard in England, and of rather uncertain status in Australia and New Zealand. It is these marginal status items which are hardest to judge. Although Australia and New Zealand tend to follow English norms for many things, it would be hard to say that an Australian or New Zealander who used *proven* was not speaking a standard variety of their English, if this were the only pointer. As such features become more widely used, they are more likely to become part of a codified norm (such norms typically – though not inevitably – being rather conservative). Where there is no codification we can judge standards only in some rather intuitive fashion. At present, there is a certain fuzziness built in to the notion of standard in non-US colonial varieties.

Exercises

1. Invent a short questionnaire to test your peers' reactions to sentences including phrases like *you and I* and *you and me*. Test it on some students (preferably not students studying English or Linguistics), and compare your results with the suggestions made in the text and with the results gained by others. Can you explain any variation in responses?

2. Make an audio tape of approximately ten minutes of *Eastenders* and *Neighbours* or any other two programmes which have speakers of non-standard London variety and speakers of a southern hemisphere variety. Alternatively, do the same for a Canadian and a US television show. Make a list of similarities and differences in pronunciation between the two varieties.

3. Is there a standard Australian English (or New Zealand English or South African English) independent of British English? Is there a standard Canadian English independent of both British and US English?

4. Read the discussion of countable and uncountable nouns in any grammar of English, and decide how far your own usage reflects the variety described in the grammar. Do you use a standard variety as far as this feature is concerned?

Recommendations for reading

On the whole notion of standard, Milroy and Milroy (1985) is recommended. On non-standard grammar in Britain, Cheshire *et al.* (1989) is the best place to start. Many descriptions of individual varieties of English make some comment on standard and non-standard in the colonies, for example Collins (1989) and Newbrook (2001) on grammatical features of Australian English. There is some elementary discussion of variable standards in Bauer (1994b).

Discussion of the exercises

Chapter 1

1. The point of the question is that you cannot simply guess, you have to investigate sources of historical information – histories of English, historical dictionaries and the like. In the particular cases chosen in the question the facts are as follows:

a) Canadian raising: It is often commented that Canadian raising is not Canadian and may not be raising. A similar phenomenon is found in much of the northern USA and in a small area in the fens in England. Nevertheless, the Canadian phenomenon is probably independent of the English one, and comments about it are found from the late 1930s onwards. It thus seems that this is a very recent phenomenon (Chambers 1989) and not colonial lag.

b) *Did you eat yet?*: This is a question on which it is difficult to get good data. The most significant-looking piece of data I have found is that Strevens (1972) fails to mention this syntactic difference between British and American varieties of English, while Quirk *et al.* (1985: 194) do draw attention to this American preference. If this reflects genuine difference, it suggests that it is a recent development in American English, and not colonial lag. Better evidence might arise from finding the two constructions in novels, films, plays, etc. written earlier in the twentieth century, or from finding discussions of these constructions in English language teaching texts from both sides of the Atlantic.

c) *Biscuit*: The *OED* is of remarkably little help in dating the advent of sweet biscuits, providing only one citation (dated 1870) for the modern British usage where *biscuit* is used mainly for a sweet biscuit. Still it is clear that biscuits were not always sweet in Britain (think of ship's biscuits, for example), which implies that British usage has changed. The US usage preserves an older sense. This is colonial lag.

2. You should be able to hear some differences, but if you cannot, you should think about why that might be. For instance, does one of the speakers use a variety which you perceive as being lower class or otherwise unworthy of imitation? Do you dislike one of the people? Have you never spoken to anyone with that particular accent before? Are you failing to hear differences which are actually present? The features that you change ought to be features you are not only aware of, but which you feel typify the accent of your interlocutor. Pronouncing /r/ in words like *car* and *cart* is far more usual for a non-rhotic speaker talking to a speaker of standard US English than, say, pronouncing *cot* and *caught* with the same vowel. Note that the pronunciation of /r/ is also supported by the spelling.

3. The initial <v> in *fog* and <z> in *sober*, and the vowels in *go* and *mother* represent matters which are entirely to do with pronunciation, and thus accent.

The plural form of *eye*, the use of the second person singular, the use of *thee* in subject position, the use of *as* to introduce a relative clause, the use of the adjectival form *sober* rather than adverbial *soberly* and the use of *Never God made* in place of the modern *Never did God make* (or *God never made*) are all dialect forms, being matters of grammar. There are no instances of dialect vocabulary in this passage (unless *sober* is taken to be one). A few lines further on, though, Blackmore introduces the word *goyal*, defined as 'a long trough among wild hills, falling towards the plain country', which is also a matter of dialect.

4. In the English cases, rhoticity is less prestigious than non-rhoticity, just the converse of the New York situation. Yet the reasons are the same in both places: the national standard pronunciation is the one which offers the prestige. However, if the same feature can have high prestige in one place and low prestige in another, it implies that what is considered 'good' English is not a matter of the linguistic form itself, but a matter of social judgement. Rhoticity as a phenomenon is neither good nor bad.

Chapter 2

1. There are a number of points that could be made about Figure 2.4. The most obvious one is that the outside circle in the figure lists varieties of different kinds. There are purely regional varieties (and these are the only varieties listed in South Asia and Africa), but also social varieties

(such as BBC English), varieties which are not really independent (such as *franglais*), and contact varieties (such as Tok Pisin), alongside native-speaker varieties. In effect, at least four circles are needed, with social varieties providing a circle outside the regional varieties. The result is that the sectors on the diagram are not all exactly equivalent. You may also have found other points worthy of comment.

2. First we need to realise that [ʊ] is perceived as being a northern variant of [ʌ] in England, so that the two are, on some level, equivalent pronunciations: *cup* is pronounced with [ʌ] in the south, but with [ʊ] in the north, even though both use [ʊ] in words like *push*. Then we need to note that the English pronunciation with [ʌ] or [ʊ] is largely from the eastern counties, while the western counties have the standard [ɪ] vowel in this position. Since the Massachusetts area of the USA was settled from the eastern counties of England, it is not surprising that [ʌ] should have been the most widespread variant there, and adopted as a norm, while settlers further south would have come from western counties, where [ɪ] was (and remains) the norm. You can see on the North American map that attestations of [ʌ] fade out as you move south and west, away from the area of original eastern counties settlement.

3. The alternative would be that New Zealand English is a direct descendant of English English, parallel to Australian English (and also South African English which is not shown in Figure 2.2).

For the most part, similar predictions would follow from either hypothesis:

- The grammar of the two varieties should be very similar, either because New Zealand English has not yet had much time to diverge from Australian English or because the two derive from basically the same English English grammar.
- The vocabulary should be similar except where loans from Maori in New Zealand and Aboriginal languages in Australia are concerned. This is either because New Zealand English vocabulary is fundamentally the same as Australian English vocabulary, with just some very recent differences, or because both derive from the same range of British vocabulary.
- Pronunciation should be fairly similar. This is either because New Zealand English pronunciation is Australian English pronunciation which has had a relatively short time to diverge from its parent, or because both New Zealand and Australian English pronunciations derive from mixtures of similar speakers at approximately the same

time – and because New Zealand English is in any case influenced by Australian English as its closest neighbour.

The differences are more difficult to be precise about:

- Since the mixture of people who settled in Australia was not the same as the mixture of people who settled in New Zealand (for example there were no penal colonies in New Zealand; the first settlers in New Zealand tended to come from rural not urban backgrounds) there should be some observable results of the different mixtures if we have two parallel developments. Unfortunately, it is virtually impossible to say what those differences should be because we do not have enough detailed information, and thus it is impossible to judge whether the observed differences between Australian and New Zealand Englishes could be caused by the different population mixes.
- There is some Australian English vocabulary which is not widely used in Britain but which is nevertheless found in New Zealand. It is argued in Bauer (1994a) that this is sufficient to make a case for New Zealand English being derived from Australian English, but the point is controversial and the relevant words could be later loans from Australian English into New Zealand English.

Chapter 3

1.

Word	Place used	Meaning
bayou	USA	marshy part of a river
caribou	Canada	kind of reindeer
dingo	Australia	wild dog
Eskimo	Canada	the aboriginal people of northern Canada, Alaska, Greenland (now usually *Inuit*); their language (now usually *Inuktitut*)
hickory	USA	tree with tough wood bearing edible nuts
kangaroo	Australia	any member of the family of marsupials having long feet, short forelimbs, a long tail for balance
kauri	New Zealand	tree with hard wood
kookaburra	Australia	large kingfisher

Word	Place used	Meaning
masonja	South Africa	mopani worm
minnerichi	Australia	tree with curling bright red bark; the tough wood from the tree
mobola	South Africa	plum-like fruit; the tree on which it grows
moose	Canada	type of large deer; elk
mulla mulla	Australia	pussy tail; a shrub with a large, fluffy flower head
pichou	Canada	lynx
quagga	South Africa	various types of zebra
raccoon	USA, Canada	small nocturnal carnivore, with mask-like markings on the face
sassafras	USA	small tree with aromatic leaves and bark
skunk	USA, Canada	cat-sized carnivore, related to weasels, known for its black and white markings and its powerful stink
squash	USA, Canada	kind of pumpkin eaten as a vegetable
toboggan	Canada	sledge
toetoe	New Zealand	pampas grass
tsamma	South Africa	a trailing plant of the Kalahari; the melon that grows on it
tsetse	South Africa	a biting fly which transmits sleeping sickness
tuatara	New Zealand	lizard-like reptile
tui	New Zealand	song bird

2. You may find sets like the following:

aubergine	eggplant		
bap	bread roll	bun	roll
batter cake	drop scone	pancake	pikelet
biscuit	cookie		
candy	lolly	spice	sweet
chips	french fries		
chips	chippies	crisps	
courgette	zucchini		
dark chocolate	plain chocolate		
French beans	string beans		

ground meat	hamburger	mince	
jam	jelly		
jello	jelly		
lemon cheese	lemon curd	lemon honey	
liquor	spirits		
porterhouse	sirloin		
mineral (water)	pop	soda	soft drink

Sometimes, these are not easily distinguished by area. For example, *courgette* and *zucchini* are both found in New Zealand, usually with no meaning difference, though some people distinguish in terms of size. *Cookie* is used in many areas outside North America, but in those areas means a special kind of biscuit; in North America a cookie is not a kind of biscuit. You may also have listed words which are differentiated by being dialectal variants within one country (for instance, *spanish* is used in parts of Britain for 'liquorice'). What is the difference, if any, between variation between nations and dialectal variation within one nation?

3. The passage is taken from Terry Pratchett's *The Last Continent* (New York: HarperTorch, 1999: 57–8). This is a fantasy novel, set in the Discworld version of a continent very like Australia. The resonances of Australian English (*boomerang, mate, tucker, beaut*) are thus entirely deliberate. Yet the passage is written by an Englishman, and could thus be said to be written in the English of England. Alternatively, it might be claimed that this is actually a representation of the English (or other language?) of the Discworld. The point may appear trivial, but is not. We recognise various items in this particular text as being Australian, yet to the extent that it is written in Australian English at all, it is written in a copy of Australian English. On the one hand this relates to the nature of pretence (when film stars play roles where they adopt an accent which is not their own, do they really speak the variety of English which their characters are supposed to be speaking?), on the other it relates to the nature of something like 'Australian English': does Australian English exist except in the actions of Australians? Is Australian English purely a matter of vocabulary choice? Can we really distinguish Australian English from English used to discuss Australia?

4. There are too many options here to tell what you are likely to have found, but consider the pair *pants/trousers*. *Trousers* is still not much used in the USA and Canada, but elsewhere *pants* has been encroaching on the territory of *trousers* for over fifty years. However, there is no simple replacement of one by the other. *Pants* has come in stealthily through

fixed phrases such as *toreador pants, ski pants, pant(s) suit,* and is probably still used more for women's garments than for men's. The development is only imperfectly reflected in the various editions of *The Concise Oxford Dictionary.* In the fifth edition (1964) *pants* is defined as '(Chiefly US) trousers; ... (shop) long tight drawers'. In the sixth edition (1976) that is amended to 'trousers or slacks; ... underpants' with further reference to *pants suit* and *bore/scare the pants off* and *with one's pants down.* And in the eighth edition (1990), the development is apparently reversed, so that it reads '*Brit* underpants or knickers. ... *US* trousers or slacks' with the same further examples.

5. There are similarities in the sense that the words listed refer to facets of Jewish culture for which there are not standard English words (a Jewish funeral is clearly perceived as being different in kind from a non-Jewish funeral). What is missing (and this is a major difference from the colonial situation) is words for flora and fauna. The reason is obvious: there were no flora and fauna in North America at the time of arrival of the Jewish settlers for which they had a name and the local north Americans did not. You can try the same exercise with borrowings from any language into English: either think up your own examples, or search the etymology section of *The Oxford English Dictionary,* or find some word-lists from any good history of the English language.

Chapter 4

1. The main point which should emerge from this exercise is how rare most of the relevant constructions are, and thus how much text you have to read through to find examples. This is, of course, relevant in explaining why the variation should occur where it does. How would you explain the correlation? In deciding whether the variation is in the expected direction, you need to be very careful with variation where Variety A allows variants x and y but Variety B allows only y: if y occurs in your texts for both A and B you may be surprised at the result, even though it is one of the predicted outcomes. Trudgill and Hannah (1994) are particularly good at drawing attention to such cases.

2. The alternatives that are presented below are not necessarily exhaustive, and the national markings given are suggestive rather than definitive, suggested by observation, by handbooks such as Trudgill and Hannah (1984), Todd and Hancock (1986), Benson *et al.* (1986: 21–3) and by dictionaries. Frequently such sources are limited to differences between British and American usage, and it may not be clear how these

generalise to other varieties. Lack of marking acknowledges the variation without attributing it to differences between national standards. I have added comments where necessary. The symbol 'Ø' means 'zero', that is, all prepositions may be omitted.

a)	in	at
b)	Ø	on (my children used this at school in New Zealand, but it is not general in adult language)
c)	Ø (UK)	from (US)
d)	Ø (UK)	from (US)
e)	out (US)	out of (UK)
f)	in (UK)	on (US)
g)	in (US)	for (UK)
h)	off (UK)	off of (US)
i)	to (UK)	toward(s) (UK) (it is not clear whether the same variation is found outside the UK)
j)	at	in
k)	in/on	under (Aus, NZ)
l)	with	to
m)	of	Ø (this option is mainly restricted to oral usage, but is now spreading into written usage, particularly in the USA)

3. The question assumes that there is a clear colonial variant and a clear Home variant; this may not always be true. In any case, in many instances the answer will be unclear: *Did you eat yet?* seems simpler than *Have you eaten yet?* only in not requiring a past participle form *eaten* – no great gain. It might seem less simple in over-riding the 'present relevance' effect which the perfect is usually required for. *Be in (the) hospital* seems no simpler one way or the other. *Did you used to* is probably simpler than *Used you to* (despite being marginally longer) in that it makes *used* more consistently like a main verb (it takes *to* like a main verb already).

4. If you suggest using texts, you run into problems (a) and (b). If you suggest asking speakers directly, you run into problem (c). Perhaps the best option would be to present speakers with some very restricted scenarios, and ask them to write down their responses or tick one preferred option from a short list of possible responses. For instance: 'You go to the fish shop and look round, but you cannot see any cod, although that shop is famous for its fresh cod. You ask the fishmonger: "…"' (with either a blank left, as here, or a series of options such as '(a) Have you any fresh cod?, (b) Do you have any fresh cod?' and so on. Interviews and writing are both likely to produce fairly formal language, which deals with (c) to some extent; writing a tight scenario can go some

way to dealing with (b); and using a questionnaire deals with (a). You can probably think of other problems with this method, though. You might like to try it with a small number of questions and just a few interviewees to see whether it would work or not.

Chapter 5

1. *Tire Centre* must be a Canadian spelling, because only in Canada do we find the North American variant <tire> alongside the final <re> in words like *centre.*

2. The passage is taken from *The Sydney Morning Herald* of 9 August 1999, p. 14. The ellipses are to avoid wordings which give away the Australian context without reference to the spelling. However, the spelling is sufficient to make clear that this is an Australian text. First the use of <ise> in *subsidised* and the use of <re> in *theatre* guarantee that the text is not North American in origin. The initial <i> in *inquiry* is, these days, not significant as to origin. While British texts still prefer the <e> spelling, both are used there, and the <e> spelling is not used in the US. Finally, we have *Labor,* which, while it could be North American on its own, cannot be when it co-occurs with the other markers, and so shows the text to be Australian.

3. Some parts of the task would be easy, in particular the lexical differences such as *grey/gray* which are fairly well maintained. It would probably be impossible to do the job completely, though, since there is so much variation on both sides. Given <ize> in an American text, it is not absolutely certain that it should be made British by changing it to <ise> – not only because of words like *supervise,* but because there is free choice in British English between the two in words like *naturalise.* Since British spellers can write *biased* as well as *biassed,* and American spellers can vary between *kidnaping* and *kidnapping,* there is no simple way to get from 'the' British version to 'the' American version or vice versa, unless you are willing to be extremely prescriptive about what is permitted in the output.

4. *I like to fantasise (i) that someone does me the sizeable (ii) honour (iii) of providing me with a travelling (iv) scholarship to visit the Centre (v) for Gypsy (vi) Studies.* (i) <ize> is acceptable everywhere, so no other changes would be needed. (ii) A version with no <e> after the <z> is acceptable everywhere, so no other changes would be needed. (iii) The <or> spelling is possible in Australia as well as in North America, so no other

changes would be necessary to make this a consistent text. (iv) The use of single <l> is North American, so we would have to change *fantasise, honour* and *centre* to make a consistent text. (v) *Center* is only North American (especially US), and so *fantasise, honour* and *travelling* would have to be changed to make this a consistent text. (vi) *Gipsy* with an <i> is much more likely to be American than British, but could be either, so that nothing else would have to be changed to make a consistent text.

5. In some cases it may be possible to read a whole book without the spelling giving absolutely clearcut information on its origin, although some relatively common words like *centre* or *colour* are likely to appear. The topic, if not the text type, is likely to be a big influence: something discussing the honours system will give many clues in the form of the word *honour*, if not in other ways. The same is true with vocabulary: a work on cars is likely to be more readily identifiable as either British or American than a work on geophysics – at least where the vocabulary is concerned.

Chapter 6

1. If you take a phrase such as *The bicycle is at my friend's house tonight; I've lent it to him*, there is nothing in the phonemes or in the distribution of phonemes or in the pronunciation of individual lexical items which would tell you specifically about the origin of a speaker who uttered it. Nonetheless, you would probably easily identify a person who spoke just those few words as coming from the US, Canada, England, Australia, New Zealand or South Africa, if you were attuned to those varieties. This suggests that the most important feature is the phonetic realisation of the particular sounds. Other things may be easier to talk about, and possibly more convincing, but the primary evidence will be in the realisation.

2. Differences in stress (RP *'croquet* vs. GA *cro'quet*; RP *'harass* vs. GA and NZ *ha'rass*, and so on); differences in intonation (see Chapter 7.3 for discussion of one such case; many varieties keep pitch relatively low and level until they reach the important word in an intonation phrase, while RP frequently jumps up on the first stressed syllable, and then falls towards the important word); differences in voice quality (ordinary language words like 'twang' and 'drawl' often refer to such differences); differences in speed, rhythm, precision of articulation, and a number of others.

3. Clearly I cannot answer for your particular accent. What is important is that you should find that the major differences fit under the headings discussed in the chapter or in the answer to question (2) above.

4. a) This is a matter of distribution: the PALM vowel is more restricted in these varieties and never occurs before a nasal + obstruent cluster.

b) This is lexical distribution: there is no generalisable pattern about the FACE ~ TRAP alternation to be captured.

c) This is a matter of phonemic systems: there is a THOUGHT – LOT merger in many North American varieties, as discussed in the text.

d) This is a matter of phonetic realisation: the quality of the Australian FACE vowel overlaps with the quality of the RP PRICE vowel, yet FACE and PRICE remain distinct in Australian English.

e) This is lexical distribution, it is purely a matter concerning this lexical item.

f) This is probably a neutralisation sub-case of distribution: the NEAR vowel and the FLEECE vowel fail to contrast before /l/. Do you make this distinction? Do you know people who do?

Chapter 7

1. It can be hard to discover whether things are or are not Americanisms in origin. *The Oxford English Dictionary* is a good source of information, and consulting different British and American dictionaries, as well as specific works which address the problem, can be helpful. You may discover that there is a popular, and as one American recently put it 'journalistic sense of *Americanism* (which, in Britain, is often applied to any usage the writer finds distasteful)' (Bailey 2000: 613). For the serious student of language, this approach is not appropriate, though it is appropriate to ask why such attitudes should exist and what they tell us about the social and political situation in which the English language is spoken. Some research done recently in New Zealand suggests that young speakers are not particularly worried by Americanisms, and that it is older speakers who find them in some ways threatening. This may or may not apply elsewhere in the world.

2. There are many possible ways of trying to prove this, most of which involve the creation or use of a corpus of some kind. For example, it might be possible to look at several British and American legal or other

administrative texts from two or more different periods (including at least the beginning and the end of the twentieth century, since Visser suggests the rise of the construction is a twentieth-century phenomenon). The proof of American influence would have to come from considering some earlier texts. Was the construction in use in mid- or late nineteenth-century Britain? Did the increase in the use of the construction occur in the United States clearly before the increase began in Britain? Even then, results would be suggestive rather than definitive. Denison (1998: 264) suggests that the rebirth of the subjunctive in British English may not be due to external influence at all. I know of no study that has considered all this in detail.

3. Many examples are provided by people such as Benson *et al.* (1986), Todd and Hancock (1986), Trudgill and Hannah (1994), and a host of other works, including the dictionaries mentioned in the Recommendations for reading section of Chapter 3.

4. One experiment carried out in New Zealand (Bayard 1989) found that American variants such as *drapes* and *flashlight* were likely to be seen as more prestigious than their British equivalents *curtains* and *torch*. Your answer will depend upon the particular pairs of words you chose and on the kind of English your informants use. There is no particular reason to suppose that New Zealand reactions will be found elsewhere: for some words it might be just the other way round in the USA!

Chapter 8

1. Your time line should show that the codification of American English was much faster than that of other varieties. If you include external political events on your time line – events such as the American War of Independence, Britain's membership of the European Union, military alliances for such events as the wars in Korea and Vietnam – you might discover that they have as much influence as time since settlement.

2. The answer is almost certainly partly a matter of political situation and partly a matter of time. American English has been viewed as separate for longer than New Zealand English has (if New Zealand English is viewed as separate, even today), and there was political will to view American English as separate from British English even at the beginning of the nineteenth century. The major difference is probably the temporal one, though an argument could be made on either side. It is slightly surprising that such a letter should appear giving such a clearly stated

anti-New-Zealand-English stance as late as 1983: perhaps the writer is British; perhaps the writer is middle-aged or older; certainly the writer is slightly conservative for the period. Most young New Zealanders at this time would have started to see New Zealand English as their own perfectly good variety. Of course, people's attitudes do not all change at the same rate, which is why I say 'slightly conservative': ten years earlier, such an attitude, even overtly expressed, would not have been unexpected.

3. The pronunciation ['harəsmənt] is the conservative English pronunciation. The pronunciation [hə'rasmənt] is either Scottish or American in origin. The fact that the writer thinks that the former is 'wrong' shows that a New Zealand norm has been adopted, and the conservative English norm has been rejected. Newsreaders, who are trained to speak according to English norms in New Zealand, are precisely the kind of people who would know what the English pronunciation is. They probably say ['harəsmənt] in an attempt to be correct. You could try to point this out to the writer, though you might not have any effect. Perhaps you should ask what makes a pronunciation 'wrong' or 'right'.

4. The names and the unmarked use of *maganu* seem to set this in South Africa, but it is not clear that you would want to change these things if the story were to be picked up by a newspaper in another country. The use of *long-haul buses* might be a lexical clue, and that could well be changed for consumption elsewhere. The spelling *centre* simply marks the text as coming from outside the USA. The use of *brew* might seem excessive, but is not impossible elsewhere. There is no grammar to show that this is South African English. This is a fairly typical situation: many (perhaps most) of the markers of regional origin are no more than markers of the setting of the story; extra glossing might be used if these were written about outside that area.

Chapter 9

1. You must take care in devising your questionnaire to make sure that *you and I* and *you and me* (or equivalent pronouns in other persons) occur in the historically correct and historically incorrect positions. You may get different responses if you ask people to fill in the blanks (and then a difference depending on whether you do this orally or in writing) or if you ask them which they think is 'better' or 'more formal' or 'posher'. Different methodologies may well lead to different answers, but I would be surprised if the answers you got were grossly different from the ones

presented in the text, unless you asked people of a very restricted social class.

2. Most of the benefit of this exercise is to be gained by giving it a serious try. It is a difficult exercise, and you may find yourself frustrated by an inability to write down in a suitable notation differences which you can hear. Precise details of what you will hear cannot be provided, since they may well depend on the varieties you listen to and the individual speakers involved. You can check that your observations are expected ones by looking in Wells (1982) or other descriptions of the individual varieties concerned. You must take care not to assume that one speaker is necessarily typical of the national variety in general.

3. This is the big question, and your answer may depend upon whether or not you are a speaker of the variety you have written about, and if so how your individual beliefs about your variety fit into the spectrum of beliefs discussed in Chapter 8. So your answer may reveal more about you than about any objective reality. Whatever you decide, you should have considered factors such as codification (see Chapter 8) and the kinds of factors discussed here about standard varieties in general.

4. I would expect you to agree with most of what is said about count-ability, but very possibly to differ in that you permit *less* as the opposite of *more* whether *more* is with a singular uncountable noun or a plural countable noun (*more bread, more loaves; less bread, less loaves*). There are then two questions which arise. First, is the description in the grammar you consulted still an accurate one for the variety of English it purports to describe? Second, does a minor difference from a described standard mean that something becomes non-standard? You might argue either way on either of these questions, and so your response to the original question may not be consistent with that of your classmates, even if you speak the same variety of English.

References

Adams, G. B. (1977), The dialects of Ulster. In Diarmaid Ó Muirthe (ed.), *The English Language in Ireland*, Dublin: Mercier Press, 56–70.

Aubrey, John (1975), *Brief Lives*. A modern English version edited by Robert Barber (original 1680). Woodbridge, Suffolk: Boydell.

Avis, Walter S. (ed.) (1967), *A Dictionary of Canadianisms on Historical Principles*, Toronto: Gage.

Bailey, Richard W. (1991), *Images of English. A cultural history of the language*, Ann Arbor: University of Michigan Press.

Bailey, Richard W. (2000), Review of Suzanne Romaine (ed.), *The Cambridge History of the English Language*, vol. IV (Cambridge: Cambridge University Press, 1998), *Journal of Linguistics* 36: 612–19.

Barber, Charles (1964), *Linguistic Change in Present-day English*, Edinburgh and London: Oliver and Boyd.

Bauer, Laurie (1989a), Marginal modals in New Zealand English, *Te Reo* 32: 3–16.

Bauer, Laurie (1989b), The verb 'have' in New Zealand English, *English World-Wide* 10: 69–83.

Bauer, Laurie (1994a), English in New Zealand. In R. W. Burchfield (ed.), *The Cambridge History of the English Language*. Vol. V: *English in Britain and Overseas, Origins and Developments*, Cambridge: Cambridge University Press, 382–429.

Bauer, Laurie (1994b), *Watching English Change*, London and New York: Longman.

Bauer, Laurie (1999), On the origins of the New Zealand English accent, *English World-Wide* 20: 287–307.

Bayard, Donn (1989), 'Me say that? No way!': the social correlates of American lexical diffusion in New Zealand English, *Te Reo* 32: 17–60.

Bell, Allan (1977), 'The language of radio news in Auckland.' Unpublished PhD thesis, University of Auckland.

Benor, Sarah (1999), Loan words in the English of modern orthodox Jews: Yiddish or Hebrew? In Steve S. Chang, Lily Liaw and Josef Ruppenhofer (eds), *Proceedings of the Twenty-Fifth Annual Meeting of the Berkeley Linguistics Society*, Berkeley: Berkeley Linguistics Society, 287–98.

Benson, Morton, Evelyn Benson and Robert Ilson (1986), *Lexicographic Description of English*, Amsterdam/Philadelphia: Benjamins.

Blundell, Sally (2001), Heow neow breown ceow? *NZ Listener*, 7 April: 26–8.

Branford, William (1994), English in South Africa. In R.W. Burchfield (ed.), *The Cambridge History of the English Language*. Vol. V: *English in Britain and Overseas, Origins and Developments*, Cambridge: Cambridge University Press, 430–96.

Bridenbaugh, Carl (1980), *Jamestown 1544–1699*, New York: Oxford University Press.

Burchfield, R. W. (ed.) (1994), *The Cambridge History of the English Language*. Vol. V: *English in Britain and Overseas, Origins and Developments*, Cambridge: Cambridge University Press.

Burchfield, R. W. (1996), *The New Fowler's Modern English Usage*, Oxford: Oxford University Press.

Butler, Susan (2001), Australian English – an identity crisis. In David Blair and Peter Collins (eds), *English in Australia*, Amsterdam/Philadelphia: Benjamins, 151–61.

Carney, Edward (1994), *A Survey of English Spelling*, London and New York: Routledge.

Carstairs-McCarthy, Andrew (2002), *An Introduction to English Morphology*, Edinburgh: Edinburgh University Press.

Carver, Craig M. (1987), *American Regional Dialects*, Ann Arbor: University of Michigan Press.

Cawdrey, Robert (1604), *A Table Alphabeticall*, London: Weauer.

Chambers J. K. (1989), Canadian raising: blocking, fronting, etc. *American Speech* 64: 75–88.

Chambers, J. K. (1998), Myth 15: TV makes people sound the same. In Laurie Bauer and Peter Trudgill (eds), *Language Myths*, Harmondsworth: Penguin, 123–31.

Cheshire, Jenny, Viv Edwards and Pamela Whittle (1989), Urban British dialect grammar: the question of levelling, *English World-Wide* 10: 185–225.

Chicago Manual of Style (1993), 14th edn, Chicago: University of Chicago Press.

Ching, Marvin K. L. (1982), The question intonation in assertions, *American Speech* 57: 95–107.

Collins, Peter (1989), Divided and debatable usage in Australian English. In Peter Collins and David Blair (eds), *Australian English*, St Lucia: University of Queensland Press, 138–49.

Concise Oxford Dictionary (1911), 5th edn, ed. H. W. and F. G. Fowler 1964; 6th edn, ed. J. B. Sykes 1976; 8th edn, ed. R. E. Allen 1990; 9th edn, ed. Della Thompson 1995; Oxford: Oxford University Press.

Cooper, Thomas (1565), *Thesaurus Linguae Romanae et Britannicae*, London: Wykes.

Crystal, David (1988), *The English Language*, Harmondsworth: Penguin.

Crystal, David (1995), *The Cambridge Encyclopedia of the English Language*, Cambridge: Cambridge University Press.

Crystal, David (1997), *English as a Global Language*, Cambridge: Cambridge University Press.

Delbridge, A. (ed.) (1981), *The Macquarie Dictionary*, McMahon's Point:

Macquarie Library.

Denison, David (1998), Syntax. In Suzanne Romaine (ed.), *The Cambridge History of the English Language*. Vol. 4: *1776–1997*, Cambridge: Cambridge University Press, 92–329.

Deverson, Tony (ed.) (1997), *New Zealand Pocket Oxford Dictionary*, 2nd edn, Auckland: Oxford University Press.

Dobson, E. J. (1968), *English Pronunciation 1500–1700*, 2nd edn, Oxford: Oxford University Press.

Evans, Bergen and Cornelia Evans (1957), *A Dictionary of Contemporary American Usage*, New York: Random House.

Fee, Margery and Janice McAlpine (1997), *Guide to Canadian English Usage*, Toronto: Oxford University Press.

Filppula, Markku (1999), *The Grammar of Irish English*, London and New York: Routledge.

Fowler, H. H. (1965), *A Dictionary of Modern English Usage*, 2nd edn revised by Ernest Gowers, Oxford: Oxford University Press.

Gimson, A. C. (1962), *An Introduction to the Pronunciation of English*, London: Edward Arnold. 2nd edn, 1970; 3rd edn, 1980; 4th edn, 1989; 5th edn, 1994.

Gordon, Elizabeth and Tony Deverson (1998), *New Zealand English and English in New Zealand*, Auckland: New House.

Görlach, Manfred (1987), Colonial lag? The alleged conservative character of American English and other 'colonial' varieties. Reprinted in Manfred Görlach, *Englishes*, Amsterdam/Philadelphia: Benjamins, 1991: 90–107.

Görlach, Manfred (1990a), *Studies in the History of the English Language*, Heidelberg: Winter.

Görlach, Manfred (1990b), Heteronymy in international English, *English World-Wide* 11: 239–74.

Görlach, Manfred (1991), *Introduction to Early Modern English*, Cambridge: Cambridge University Press. German original, 1978.

Grant, William (ed.) (1934–76), *Scottish National Dictionary*, Edinburgh: Riverside.

Hundt, Marianne (1998), *New Zealand English Grammar. Fact or fiction?* Amsterdam/Philadelphia: Benjamins.

James, Eric, Christopher Mahut and George Latkiewicz (1989), Investigation of an apparently new intonation pattern in Toronto English, *Information Communication* (Phonetics Laboratory, University of Toronto) 10: 11–17.

Jamieson, John (1808–25), *An Etymological Dictionary of the Scottish Language*, Edinburgh.

Johnson, Samuel (1755), *A Dictionary of the English Language*, London: Rivington.

Jones, Daniel (1918), *An Outline of English Phonetics*, 2nd edn, 1922; 3rd edn, 1932; 4th edn, 1934; 5th edn, 1936; 6th edn, 1939; 7th edn, 1949; 8th edn, 1956; 9th edn, 1960; 9th edn, amended 1972, Cambridge: Heffer.

Jonson, Ben (1640), *The English Grammar*, London.

Kachru, Braj B. (1985), Standards, codification and sociolinguistic realism: the English language in the outer circle. In Randolph Quirk and H. G.

Widdowson (eds), *English in the World*, Cambridge: Cambridge University Press, 11–30.

Kallen, Jeffrey L. (1997), Irish English: context and contacts. In Jeffrey L. Kallen (ed), *Focus on Ireland*, Amsterdam/Philadelphia: Benjamins, 1–33.

Kenyon, John S. and Thomas A. Knott (1953), *A Pronouncing Dictionary of American English*, Springfield, MA: G and C Merriam.

Kniffen, Fred B. and Henry Glassie (1966), Building in wood in the Eastern United States, *Geographical Review* 56: 40–66.

Kolb, Eduard, Beat Glauser, Willy Elmer and Renate Stamm (1979), *Atlas of English Sounds*, Bern: Francke.

Koukl, Gregory (1994), Killing abortionists. <http://www.str.org/free/commentaries/abortion/killing.htm> (accessed 2 October 2001).

Kurath, Hans and Raven I. McDavid Jr (1961), *The Pronunciation of English in the Atlantic States*, Ann Arbor: University of Michigan Press.

Labov, William (1994), *Principles of Linguistic Change: Internal factors*, Oxford and Cambridge MA: Blackwell.

Ladefoged, Peter and Ian Maddieson (1996), *The Sounds of the World's Languages*, Oxford and Cambridge MA: Blackwell.

Lanham, L.W. (1982), English in South Africa. In Richard W. Bailey and Manfred Görlach (eds), *English as a World Language*, Cambridge: Cambridge University Press, 324–52.

Larsen, Thorleif and Francis C. Walker (1930), *Pronunciation: a practical guide to American Standards*, London: Oxford University Press.

Lass, Roger (1987), *The Shape of English*, London and Melbourne: Dent.

Lass, Roger (1990), Where do extraterritorial Englishes come from? In Sylvia Adamson, Vivien Law, Nigel Vincent and Susan Wright (eds), *Papers from the 5th International Conference on English Historical Linguistics*, Amsterdam/Philadelphia: Benjamins, 245–80.

Lehrer, Tom (1965), Who's next? On *That Was the Year That Was*, Reprise Records 6179–2.

Leith, Dick (1983), *A Social History of English*, London: Routledge and Kegan Paul.

Lindquist, Hans (2000), *Livelier* or *more lively*? Syntactic and contextual factors influencing the comparsion of disyllabic adjectives. In John M. Kirk (ed.), *Corpora Galore*, Amsterdam and Atlanta GA: Rodopi, 125–32.

Lowth, Robert (1762), *A Short Introduction to English Grammar*, London.

McArthur, Tom (1987), The English languages? *English Today* 11: 9–11.

McArthur, Tom (1998), *The English Languages*, Cambridge: Cambridge University Press.

McClure, J. Derrick (1994), English in Scotland. In R. W. Burchfield (ed.), *The Cambridge History of the English Language*. Vol. V: *English in Britain and Overseas, Origins and Developments*, Cambridge: Cambridge University Press, 23–93.

McCrum, Robert, William Cran and Robert MacNeil (1986), *The Story of English*, New York: Viking.

McKinnon, Malcolm, Barry Bradley and Russell Kirkpatrick (1997), *New*

Zealand Historical Atlas, Auckland: Bateman.

McMahon, April (2002), *An Introduction to English Phonology*, Edinburgh: Edinburgh University Press.

Markham, David (1995), Supervizing supervisors LO1795. <http://world.std.com/~lo/95.06/0325.html> (accessed 10 May 2001).

Miller, Jim (2002), *An Introduction to English Syntax*, Edinburgh: Edinburgh University Press.

Milroy, James and Lesley Milroy (1985), *Authority in Language*, London: Routledge and Kegan Paul.

Montgomery, Michael (1998), Myth 9: In the Appalachians they speak like Shakespeare. In Laurie Bauer and Peter Trudgill (eds), *Language Myths*, Harmondsworth: Penguin, 66–76.

Morris, Edward E. (1898), *A Dictionary of Austral English*, London: Macmillan.

Moss, Norman (1984), *The British/American Dictionary*, London: Hutchinson.

Munro, Pamela (ed.) (1997), *UCLA Slang 3*, UCLA Occasional Papers in Linguistics 18.

Murray, Lindley (1795), *English Grammar*, York: Wilson, Spence and Mawman.

Newbrook, Mark (2001), Syntactic features and norms in Australian English. In David Blair and Peter Collins (eds), *English in Australia*, Amsterdam/Philadelphia: Benjamins, 113–32.

Orsman, H. W. (ed.) (1997), *The Dictionary of New Zealand English*, Auckland: Oxford University Press.

Orton, Harold, Stewart Sanderson and John Widdowson (1978), *The Linguistic Atlas of England*, London: Croom Helm.

Oxford English Dictionary. See Simpson and Weiner (eds) (1989).

Peters, Pam (1995), *The Cambridge Australian Style Guide*, Cambridge: Cambridge University Press.

Peters, Pam (2001), Varietal effects: the influence of American English on Australian and British English. In Bruce Moore (ed.), *Who's Centric Now?* Melbourne: Oxford University Press, 297–309.

Pettman, Charles (1913), *Africanderisms*, London: Longman.

Pratt, T. K. (1993), The hobgoblin of Canadian English spelling. In Sandra Clarke (ed.), *Focus on Canada*. Amsterdam/Philadelphia: Benjamins, 45–64.

Quinn, Heidi (2000), Variation in New Zealand English syntax and morphology. In Allan Bell and Koenraad Kuiper (eds), *New Zealand English*, Amsterdam/Philadelphia: Benjamins, 173–97.

Quirk, Randolph (1985), The English language in a global context. In Randolph Quirk and H. G. Widdowson (eds), *English in the World*, Cambridge: Cambridge University Press, 1–6.

Quirk, Randolph, Sidney Greenbaum, Geoffrey Leech and Jan Svartvik (1985), *A Comprehensive Grammar of the English Language*, London and New York: Longman.

Ramson, W. S. (ed.) (1988), *The Australian National Dictionary*, Melbourne: Oxford University Press.

Sheridan, Thomas (1780), *A General Dictionary of the English Language*, London.

Silva, Penny (ed.) (1996), *A Dictionary of South African English on Historical Principles*, Oxford: Oxford University Press.

Simpson, J. A. and E. S. C. Weiner (eds) (1989), *Oxford English Dictionary*, 2nd edn, Oxford: Oxford University Press. Also available on CD and online at <http://dictionary.oed.com/>.

Strang, Barbara M. H. (1970), *A History of English*, London: Methuen.

Strevens, Peter (1972), *British and American English*, London: Collier-Macmillan.

Sudbury, Andrea (2001), Falkland Islands English. A southern hemisphere variety? *English World-Wide* 22: 55–80.

Sussex, Roly (1999), Americanisms in Australian English, <http://www.abc.net.au/rn/arts/ling/stories/s55759.htm>

Taylor, Brian (1989), American, British and other foreign influences on Australian English since World War II. In Peter Collins and David Blair (eds), *Australian English*, St Lucia: University of Queensland Press, 225–54.

Todd, Loreto and Ian Hancock (1986), *International English Usage*, London: Croom Helm.

Trudgill, Peter (1986), *Dialects in Contact*, Oxford and New York: Blackwell.

Trudgill, Peter, Elizabeth Gordon, Gillian Lewis and Margaret Maclagan (2000), Determinism in new dialect formation and the genesis of New Zealand English, *Journal of Linguistics* 36: 299–318.

Trudgill, Peter and Jean Hannah (1994), *International English*, 3rd edn, London: Arnold.

Turner, George W. (1994), English in Australia. In R. W. Burchfield (ed.), *The Cambridge History of the English Language*. Vol. V: *English in Britain and Overseas, Origins and Developments*, Cambridge: Cambridge University Press, 277–327.

Visser, F. Th. (1963), *An Historical Syntax of the English Language*, Leiden: Brill.

Walker, John (1791), *A Critical Pronouncing Dictionary of the English Language*, London.

Watt, Dominic and Lesley Milroy (1999), Patterns of variation and change in three Newcastle vowels: is this dialect levelling? In Paul Foulkes and Gerard Docherty (eds), *Urban Voices*, London: Arnold, 25–46.

Webster, Noah (1783), *The American Spelling Book*, Hartford CT.

Webster, Noah (1823), *An American Dictionary of the English Language*, New York: Converse.

Wells, J. C. (1982), *Accents of English*, Cambridge: Cambridge University Press. 3 vols.

Weatherall, Ann, Cynthia Gallois and Jeffery Pittam (1998), Australasians identifying Australasian accents, *Te Reo* 41: 153–62.

Weiner, E. S. C. and J. M. Hawkins (1984), *The Oxford Guide to the English Language*, Oxford: Oxford University Press.

Wolfram, Walt and Natalie Schilling-Estes (1998), *American English*, Malden MA and Oxford: Blackwell.

Zvidadze, Givi (1983), *Dictionary of Contemporary American English contrasted with British English*, New Delhi: Arnold–Heinemann.

Index

Note: entries in **bold** give the place where the term is defined.